Rethinking Equal Opportunity

Rethinking Equal Opportunity

Dignity, Human Capability, and Justice

Harlan Beckley

ROWMAN & LITTLEFIELD
Lanham • Boulder • New York • London

Published by Rowman & Littlefield
An imprint of The Rowman & Littlefield Publishing Group, Inc.
4501 Forbes Boulevard, Suite 200, Lanham, Maryland 20706
www.rowman.com

86-90 Paul Street, London EC2A 4NE

British Library Cataloguing in Publication Information available

Library of Congress Cataloging-in-Publication Data

Names: Beckley, Harlan, 1943- author.
Title: Rethinking equal opportunity : dignity, human capability, and justice /
  Harlan Beckley.
Description: Lanham : Rowman & Littlefield, [2024] | Includes bibliographical
  references and index.
Identifiers: LCCN 2023051209 (print) | LCCN 2023051210 (ebook) |
  ISBN 9781538191040 (cloth) | ISBN 9781538191057 (paperback)
  | ISBN 9781538191064 (ebook)
Subjects: LCSH: Equality--Economic aspects--United States. | Equality--Social
  aspects--United States. | Discrimination--United States.
Classification: LCC HN90.S6 B425 2024 (print) | LCC HN90.S6 (ebook) |
  DDC 305.50973--dc23/eng20240307
LC record available at https://lccn.loc.gov/2023051209
LC ebook record available at https://lccn.loc.gov/2023051210

Dedicated to
Debby,
Ben,
Jon,
and Rachel

Contents

Acknowledgments

Readers of this volume will not be surprised that I believe the opportunity to write and publish it was made possible by many institutions and persons. My gratitude for this opportunity begins with the National Humanities Center in the Research Triangle Park of North Carolina, where I spent 1995–1996 working on a book on equal opportunity with a different purpose. That project targeted scholars in philosophical and theological ethics. As noted in the introduction, that work was interrupted by an invitation from John W. Elrod, then president of Washington and Lee University, to initiate an interdisciplinary program for poverty and human capability in 1997. This program was funded and nurtured by Tom and Nancy Shepherd, respectively, managing director of the Thomas H. Lee Company and Episcopal priest in the Boston area. This book would not have been possible without the support and leadership of Hank Dobin, who became Dean of the College at Washington and Lee in 2005 and provided instrumental support for the Shepherd Program. David Bradley, CEO of the National Community Action Foundation, also provided valuable multifaceted support for the Shepherd Program at Washington and Lee and for the Shepherd Higher Education Consortium on Poverty. He remains involved to this day.

I also learned from over one thousand students who participated in courses and internships with the Shepherd Program as well as from program staff and colleagues from many disciplines at Washington and Lee. These faculty colleagues advised the program and taught courses relevant to poverty and human capability. Alums from Washington and Lee—J. Larry Connolly, Richard Duke Cancelmo, Andrew Kumpuris, and Victoria Kumpuris Brown merit special mention—offered invaluable support and advice for the Shepherd Program and Consortium. From the very beginning, this consortium was supported by faculty, staff, and students from other schools. In 2012, these schools and others joined a Shepherd Higher Education Consortium on Poverty, recently directed by Timothy Diette, also a member of the Washington and Lee faculty. My qualifications for this book were made possible by all these institutions and persons.

More recently, specific colleagues and friends have nurtured the current volume so that it could merit publication by Rowman & Littlefield. Singular among them is James F. Childress, university professor emeritus at the University of Virginia, where he was a member of the Department of Religious Studies and taught biomedical ethics for many years. Jim read an earlier draft of the manuscript and recommended many vital revisions and Rowman & Littlefield as a possible publisher. Howard Pickett, current director of the Shepherd Program at Washington and Lee, and my spouse, Debby Beckley, also deserve much credit for improving early drafts of this book. Dr. Andrew Kumpuris, MD, from Little Rock, and my former student Victoria Kumpuris Brown, a senior program officer at the Robert Wood Johnson Foundation, offered insightful and encouraging comments on earlier drafts. Both are also advisors to the Shepherd Program and Consortium. Finally, Thomas Burish, recently retired provost at the University of Notre Dame and former president at Washington and Lee, graciously read the manuscript and offered advice about publicizing it for potential student and small group readers.

In addition, I have benefited from the guidance and advice of Richard Brown, the senior executive editor for religion and spirituality at Rowman & Littlefield, as well as comments by three anonymous reviewers who Richard persuaded to read and evaluate the initially submitted draft.

Without these and other persons and institutions fostering the opportunity for me to publish this book, you would not be reading it.

Introduction

The Need for a Book on
Equality of Opportunity

In a *Time* magazine cover story, Steven Brill referred to "economic opportunity" in the United States as an "empty cliché." Brill's point? Economic opportunity for all, once a generally accepted aspiration by political parties and the general public, has become a vacuous concept.

I concur with much of what Brill says; there is popular, though facile, agreement that the United States continues to offer equality of at least economic opportunity. The problem is that this popular agreement is bereft of thoughtful substance. It is empty. I believe that we need collective agreement about a more substantive conception and application of equal opportunity for all.

This observation that economic opportunity is an "empty cliché" partially forms the starting point of this book. I hope to take advantage of the widespread acceptance of equal opportunity—not merely economic opportunity, as Brill puts it—to invite readers to consider a more substantive conception of what can be an important aspect of justice in this nation.

I will explore equal opportunity—more accurately, "fair equality of opportunity"—as a norm that commands at least casual consent from many US citizens. If we can agree about what fair equality of opportunity *requires*, the shared conception could offer a collective normative principle and disposition to move us toward policies, practices, institutions, and interpersonal behavior for a more just society.

Even if our collective consent to equal opportunity is devoid of much substance, it forms a shaky platform for a more thoughtful exploration and deliberation of what equal opportunity requires of us individually and collectively. My purpose is to offer a substantive concept, principle, and disposition that can guide our thinking about justice and rescue us from an empty cliché. I shall propose meaningful content for equal opportunity as a morally, socially, politically, and science-informed conception.

While normative conceptions and principles do not entail specific policies, practices, structures, and behavior, they provide guidance that informs our collective disposition and identifies relevant social scientific information for specific applications. They can frame our collective deliberations about the structures and behaviors that can move us toward equal opportunity and even comprehensive justice. They can move us beyond vacuous consent—or polarizing assertions—to a common framework for meaningful deliberations.[1]

My proposal begins with a demur from Brill's modifier "economic." Opportunity encompasses more than economic outcomes, although economics is a significant component. Outcomes measured by income alone do not fully capture the consequences of opportunity. Persons and groups want opportunities for more than mere economic outcomes. They may want to pursue outcomes that improve their personal and group conceptions of well-being and also goals for the common good that transcend their personal well-being. For example, they may want to sacrifice increases in income and economic position for the sake of family time, involvement in community, artistic achievements and indulgences, reading and education for its own sake, or pursuit of social justice that sacrifices narrowly conceived personal well-being. I have in mind, for example, persons that sacrifice a high-profile position and income to work for nonprofits who advance education for vulnerable persons in their community. This book remains open to all of these outcomes. High income does not in itself indicate greater opportunity.

The rational and justified aims of the citizens and residents of the United States include goods beyond income, wealth, and positions in the economy. Economic outcomes often contribute to these other goals, but in some instances they compete with them. Reducing opportunity to mere economic outcomes measured only by money and position, which is unfortunately all too common, truncates and distorts opportunity's possibilities. Hence, the term "equal opportunity" used in this book refers to all the outcomes mentioned above.

My first attempt to write about equal opportunity began as a scholarly project more than twenty-five years ago at the National Humanities Center in the Research Triangle Park of North Carolina. It was to engage philosophical and religious ethicists and those deeply interested in this scholarship as applied to a just society. That work was interrupted by an invitation to direct an interdisciplinary higher education program focused on poverty. That program at Washington and Lee University, the institution where I served on the faculty beginning in 1974, included collaboration with other higher education institutions focused on poverty studies for undergraduate and professional students aspiring to a variety of careers and civic activities.[2]

I learned a great deal working with colleagues—at Washington and Lee and elsewhere—in many disciplines, as well as from students seeking to understand poverty and committed to diminishing it through their work and civic involvement. Interns from the Consortium worked in such diverse places as Dorchester Bay, Massachusetts; Camden, New Jersey; McDowell County, West Virginia; and Phillips County, Arkansas, along the Mississippi River. They interned in such diverse positions as the Harlem Children's Zone, the Dorchester Bay Economic Development Corporation, and rural tutoring programs and food banks. Each summer, we held meetings on-site with interns and local people, where they worked and ended with a conference at which the interns reported to one another and their faculty about what they were learning. Some also had some firsthand experience interacting with communities and learning from persons who often lacked opportunities. Importantly, poverty in these programs is understood broadly as the lack of means to achieved desired outcomes and not narrowly as a lack of income and material well-being.

Both students and faculty integrated our firsthand experience with readings, discussions and papers focused on ethics, various social sciences, and the causes and possible remedies for poverty. Few of us directly experienced poverty, but this multidisciplinary and firsthand-experience focus on poverty and enlarging opportunities informs this book.

Consequently, this proposal is informed by many disciplines beyond ethics, as well as by learning from firsthand engagement with persons struggling to enhance their lives through structures and interpersonal relationships that impinge on their opportunities. It is largely due to this first- and secondhand learning mediated by many students that my understanding of constraints on opportunity is not limited to low income and wealth but includes impediments to opportunities for a broad array of desired outcomes. For example, living in communities subject to racial and ethnic division, violence, drug addiction, or limited educational opportunities can subvert opportunity for life choices only tangentially related to money and income. We all observed these impediments to opportunity when we witnessed a single parent struggling to form a family without assistance for childcare or help with adequate nutrition, education, and recreation for the children. The experience of a food dessert in Camden, New Jersey, and the burden of finding public transportation to a decent grocery store are themselves learning experiences.

Although informed by many theological, philosophical, and social science scholars, this book has a very different purpose from the one I started twenty-five years ago. It is written for all who care about equal opportunity as a key concept in a system of justice. Readers may not be highly familiar with or even keenly interested in a comprehensive and deep exploration of the scholarly literature. You may, nevertheless, want to think more deeply about the vacuous cliché to which Steven Brill alludes. Perhaps such a book—informed by but not deeply ensconced in the scholarly literature—can help us engage in more examined substantive public discourse and advocacy. It may move us toward a common conception and principle of equal opportunity to which many of us—perhaps most of us—could subscribe. Perhaps this examination of opportunity can help us transcend mere partisan politics without abandoning policy considerations and political and civic effectiveness to achieve justice. We should be more focused on what equal opportunity requires than on which candidates and political party has unfairly politicized democracy.

I hope this project can help us examine views of equal opportunity (economic and beyond) that we have rather thoughtlessly adopted from our associates and culture. That is what ethics—and allied disciplines that inform and are informed by ethics—are about. We can step back from simplistic concepts such as economic or equal opportunity to be sure they cohere and are worthy of our commitment. These concepts should comport with considered observations from our experience and the data that bear on it, as well as with our reasoning in dialogue with others.[3]

NOTES

1. Widespread concurrence with some concept of equal opportunity is not universal. Christine Sypnowich, head of the Philosophy Department at Queens University in Kingston, Canada, takes exception to the prominence of equality of opportunity among contemporary egalitarian liberals. She favors a normative conception of equality of outcomes, that is to say, equal flourishing as equal well-being for all. Her view is succinctly stated in "Is Equal Opportunity Enough?" published in a "Forum" essay of the *Boston Review*, a reader-funded website at letters@bostonreview.net. See also *Equality Renewed: Justice, Flourishing and the Egalitarian Ideal* (New York and London: Routledge, 2017) for a more refined account of Sypnowich's objection to equality of opportunity as a normative principle. A refined analysis of our differences and a response to her criticisms would require deep engagement in ethical scholarship. That is not my purpose. Sypnowich objects to the affirmations of freedom of choice, responsibility, and merit in the current book. That said, my account within this proposal for fair equality of opportunity takes seriously many of her objections to equal opportunity, and she is more nuanced regarding equality of outcomes than are many of her fellow socialists. Readers attentive to scholarly debates may wish to compare and contrast my position with hers. The differences are not simple. I appreciate her insights.

2. The collaboration continues as a Higher Education Consortium on Poverty. The interdisciplinary program at Washington and Lee flourishes as a highly popular minor for students with multiple majors advancing toward many different professional trajectories and civic interests. Colleges and universities in the Consortium have advanced poverty studies in similar ways.

3. I hope readers will be intrigued to learn from, quarrel with, and even commit to a conception of equal opportunity more pertinent to justice than an "empty cliché."

Chapter 1

The Elements

Let's begin with a broad overview of the ingredients that constitute a conception of fair equality of opportunity. We can then move on to particulars.

As I suggested, the conception of equal opportunity proposed here incorporates elements well beyond the bromide that standard economic positions should be open to the most qualified without prejudices regarding characteristics such as race, independent of qualifications. Certainly, just opportunities should differentiate between qualifications for a position and prejudices rooted in nepotism, race, ethnicity, national identity, gender, or sexual orientation. However, determining appointments based on short-term economic productivity does not adequately respect fair equality of opportunity. Even efforts to focus merit beyond narrowly conceived economic productivity (e.g., demonstrated contributions to community or envisioned benefits to many stakeholders) ignore much of what equal opportunity should consider.

We will consider at least two matters beyond qualifications for benefiting the economy.

1. *What achievements and values do persons actually desire and what positions (e.g., educator, artist, parent, community member, entrepreneur, civic leader) correspond to these values and desires?*
2. *How are qualifications or merits for these varied positions developed?*

Regarding the first matter, not all persons seek to maximize economic outcomes. Some want time for family and friends or for leisure and intellectual development as well as to contribute to civic life as much or more than to receive more income, accumulate more wealth, or achieve job prestige. Does the structure of society enable these choices?

Regarding the second matter, does society enable persons to become qualified for the positions and the accompanying outcomes they desire? A society that does not enable all persons to become qualified for positions they might desire does not provide equal opportunity. It is not sufficient simply to offer positions based on established qualifications. An equal opportunity society must also provide the means for persons to become qualified for the positions they want to pursue. In fact, persons cannot even choose what outcomes they desire without the means to make an informed choice.

My first encounter with the view that equal opportunity cannot be captured by a simple view that positions are open to the most qualified occurred years ago reading John Rawls, the outstanding twentieth-century moral philosopher who preferred the conception of "fair equality of opportunity." Rawls and his scholarly critics have influenced social justice and shaped it to extend far beyond appointing the most qualified person for a position. They agree that equal opportunity considers social structures, policies, and law and politics—that is, factors in addition to non-prejudicial judgments about which applicants are most qualified. For Rawls, "fair" opportunity requires that society provide persons in pluralistic societies with *choice about the outcomes* they pursue (encapsulated in his principle of liberty) and *supports persons to develop qualifications* and other means for the ends they seek.[1]

Rawls's claim can be illustrated by imagining the simple example of a person who grows up in a neighborhood that does not offer an adequate education that could enable her to choose whether to seek employment in a profession demanding skills that only a good education can offer. She is not denied opportunity merely by prejudice based on gender. She does lack qualifications for skilled professional positions. She cannot even imagine them, but neither would we want to claim she was offered an equal opportunity with another person whose education permitted her to choose whether to pursue such employment and become qualified for it.

My understanding of fair equality of opportunity now transcends John Rawls and is informed by other ethicists and social scientists.

Opportunity depends on more than adequate education. It requires capabilities cultivated by family, neighborhoods, and societal structures.[2]

OPPORTUNITY FOR WHAT?

Let's first consider freedom for individuals or collaborative groups (e.g., families or religious associations) to pursue the values, goals, and well-being they choose. As this book unfolds, readers will note that I believe that some associations (e.g., families, civic and religious groups) may have common goals for their members while respecting individuals within the associations. (Respect for other individuals prohibits violence and harassment and encourages and promotes individual autonomy and independence.) However, individuals make choices and develop capabilities as part of families and associations (e.g., a religious institution or civic organization), and these associations are necessary means for individual autonomy and opportunity (e.g., nurturing shared values). Individual autonomy does not occur apart from associates with shared values that nurture individuals. For example, without a family that nurtures values to which we consent, we are not capable of affirming distinctive preferences.

To be sure, some of these groups curtail individual opportunity or lead to domestic violence or child abuse, but I will not celebrate opportunity as a solely individual achievement independent of strong associations. Opportunity includes the possibility of forming collaborative values and actions and requires associations of various kinds to nurture the qualifications and the means individuals need to seek their own outcomes. We do not, for example, come to value education or leisure time for ourselves without formation in civic organizations or religious institutions. Hence, individual opportunity, including the freedom to choose the outcomes we desire, is not possible without associations enabling us, even if some groups sometimes unjustly restrict some individual freedoms.

I reiterate and emphasize: The end of opportunity cannot be limited to maximizing income and wealth or to any other assumed conceptions of what constitutes a person's well-being or achievements. Persons and groups will choose to pursue different outcomes as opportunity allows for this freedom. Some will seek more income through productive work; others will prefer additional leisure time or civic involvement over greater income.

In addition, equal opportunity goes beyond accounting for persons' preferences. It must also offer them, insofar as possible, the means necessary, that is, capability, to acquire qualifications for the ends compatible with their preferences. That does not mean that society offers persons the capability to pursue any end they choose, but it should offer the capability for persons to pursue ends compatible with their preferences and equal opportunities for others. Equal opportunity does not require that each of us has the capability to pursue any end; it does require that we have the capability to pursue equally valuable ends consonant with reasonable desires. See below for the differences and similarities among me, Ernie Banks,[3] and Robert Louis Gates Jr. I never had the capability to qualify for the outcomes that Ernie Banks or Robert Louis Gates Jr. achieved, but I believe I did have the capability to qualify for equally valuable, though different outcomes. I had the means to become qualified. That is not to say that I achieved functioning commensurate with either of them.

Considered together, offering choice about outcomes and providing the means to achieve those outcomes place limits on unrestricted freedom of choice.

These limits on individual and group freedom exist for two reasons.

First, we are not permitted to choose ends for which we cannot effectively become qualified, even if our capabilities are fostered by society. Consider, for example, an insistence that I should have the freedom to become a professional athlete. Efforts to make this end possible despite my limited innate capacities would deprive others of the capability to pursue ends for which they are, with appropriate nurturing, naturally enabled to achieve. Efforts to enable me to become an all-star shortstop for the Chicago Cubs, no matter how much I wanted it, would have been fruitless and may have deprived Ernie Banks of the support he needed to attain that end. Efforts to enable individual freedom to choose outcomes can protect a range of valuable outcomes available for everyone without guaranteeing all the freedom to achieve whatever whimsical desire they wish.

Second, individuals and groups are not permitted to indulge themselves in liberties that deprive others of capability they need for a range of outcomes. For example, opportunity for any outcome requires a minimal level of health, even if excellent health is not the pinnacle of a person's well-being. We are all obligated to support the health others need to be capable of functioning in the activities they desire.

Similarly, opportunity requires that all persons have outlets for satisfying activity, even if a particular kind of work is not the singular end of opportunity. We cannot all become civic or political leaders, but we can all have the capability for a satisfying vocation to which we readily consent. We may have to make sacrifices to ensure that our fellow citizens can qualify for a position they find satisfying. For example, we should be willing to pay taxes for others to have jobs and recreational activities they find meaningful. Individuals should not be free to amass income and wealth that deprives others of public support for work and activities to which they can and should have access.

These opportunities assume restricting some individual liberties in order to foster the capability of others for opportunities to pursue their preferred outcomes. We may be required to sacrifice the liberty for some income or other outcomes to ensure others' equal opportunity. For example, I am not free to reject paying taxes or ignore others guaranteed positions of responsibility to indulge my own wishes.

In a fair-equality-of-opportunity society, individuals are not free to ignore their obligations to societal structures that support others' freedom and capability to make choices and to become qualified to execute those choices. Our obligation requires helping others foster capability to execute outcomes consistent with their preferences and given capacities.

In sum, our freedom to choose the desired outcomes of opportunity are limited by what is required for fair opportunity and justice for others. As simple examples, fair opportunity does not include freedom to employ favorite applicants who lack qualifications; to smoke tobacco in all settings or to spread infectious diseases, for example, coronavirus, in a public setting; to betray a stable family life upon which vulnerable members depend for their opportunities. Sometimes the limits need to be legally enforced, for example, vaccination or masking mandates. On other occasions, public moral guidance and incentives for voluntary compliance—for example, wearing masks during an airborne infectious pandemic—may be the most effective and practical means for restraining individual liberties. In all cases, prudent structural arrangements and self-imposed restraints are needed to promote the means for all persons

Chapter 1

to choose and execute equally valuable but not identical desired ends. These structural arrangements and self-restraints necessarily curtail individual freedoms—for example, my freedom to ignore testing and mask or vaccination requirements—when that freedom has been shown to jeopardize the health of my family and fellow citizens.

APPROXIMATING EQUAL OPPORTUNITY IN THE UNITED STATES

We need to know what we can do to approximate equal capability for individuals, at least for US citizens and documented residents, to pursue the ends they choose.[4] Given the complexity of fair equality of opportunity providing the means to become qualified to pursue desired outcomes, we must begin by considering when and how we fall short of this approximation.

As previously observed, determining who achieves their choices based on qualifications alone is grossly insufficient. It neglects the means to develop qualifications. Offering employment to the most qualified for a position does not satisfy society's obligation to provide the education, experience, and social basis of self-respect to become qualified. And it does not meet the requirement to ensure a satisfying position for all persons. A society that outlaws discrimination based on factors irrelevant to qualifications for positions may still fall far short of fair opportunity. An individual lacking a minimally decent education or adequate healthcare also lacks fair opportunity when she falls short of the educational or health qualifications for a position. A society that fails to nurture ample means to develop the capability necessary to pursue desired outcomes does not provide real opportunity, even if it focuses only on relevant qualifications for a position.

How do we know when this unfair opportunity occurs? Statistical data help answer this question. Differential crucial outcomes for various demographic groups—by gender, race and ethnicity, social economic status, recent immigrants, persons disabled in some way, and in specific geographic locations—is a good place to start. Nothing endemic to these groups makes individuals within the groups disproportionately fall short of qualifications for most positions they prefer. Social science can help reveal structural and cultural injustices that thwart or fail to foster opportunities for some members of these groups. If, for example, African Americans, Native Americans, or Latinx do not complete higher education degrees in roughly equal proportions to White Americans, we can be confident that the former are deprived of the capability to become qualified. Data and qualitative observations—for example, reluctance to aggressively recruit African Americans for some positions—can reveal why this is so. We will return to this issue in response to the Harvard and University of North Carolina Supreme Court case about affirmative action in higher education admissions.

Remedies cannot be effective unless we identify the deficiencies that lead to thwarting opportunity because they fail to foster capabilities. It may be, among other specific deficiencies, passive recruitment practices, poor early education, disadvantaged neighborhoods, or something in the process of seeking higher education. We should seek to identify these deficiencies rather than be satisfied with the general observations that certain groups are encumbered by their history if we are to provide effective opportunities by bolstering capabilities.

These obstacles are similar for poor and geographically isolated individuals and for disabled persons. The disability—usually not of their own making[5]—hinders results they would desire and achieve if society appropriately fostered their capability. Disabilities can often be eliminated or greatly diminished. Disabilities are rarely intractable. Targeted economic policies can overcome geographic and poor household disadvantages. These impediments to opportunity can be reduced if not eradicated. Fair opportunity requires that society take specific action to do so.

Realizing fair opportunity requires refined analysis to determine which segments of these groups lack equal capability and how these injustices can be remedied. We can expect a proportionate number from each group not to choose outcomes that many do prefer. Another portion may also fail to take responsibility for the outcomes they do choose. These persons are not denied fair equality of opportunity, but we should not anticipate that a disproportionate number of individuals in a racial or other disadvantaged group, or among disabled persons, to choose ends contrary to those others desire and achieve. For example, some individual Black or disabled persons may choose not to pursue a higher education degree, or they may be irresponsible in pursuing that educational end. There is no reason, however, to assume that Black or disabled persons disproportionately choose to reject this common educational goal or are disproportionately irresponsible in executing their desire. When this disproportion occurs, we must look for the specific reasons that impede capability.

Hence, if a higher proportion of a racial or disabled group does not complete a higher education degree, this data indicates that society falls short of fair equality of opportunity. No characteristic of these groups indicates that a higher proportion of individuals in the groups will not choose or responsibly execute their desire for a higher education degree. There will be individuals within the group, in roughly equal proportion to other groups, who don't choose higher education as a desired outcome and others who fail to take responsibility for executing an outcome they choose. These persons have not been denied fair opportunity; however, they will rarely or never be a disproportionate number relative to other groups.

In these cases, society fails to nurture the capability for these persons to choose and achieve the outcomes in question. Fair equality of opportunity—that is, opportunity supported by positive support for specific capabilities to become qualified and to achieve—does not exist for them.

Science and social science are necessary to identify the specific structural encumbrances to developing capability. These encumbrances may differ among groups treated unjustly. For example, the impediments might be discriminatory policing and justice systems, inadequate or discriminatory healthcare and public health practices, and/or class or racially segregated housing that undermines adequate and equal education. For disabled persons, the impediment might be either a failure of society to support therapeutic efforts to moderate the disability or a failure to adjust positions to accommodate disabilities of persons otherwise fully able to produce in the positions they seek. For example, the encumbrance may be a failure to provide communication tools designed for persons with poor eyesight rather than correcting the eyesight deficiencies with which many persons are naturally afflicted. Note again that the issue is not merely whether these persons are qualified but whether society fosters the specific capability for them to become qualified and achieve the ends they desire by conducting themselves responsibly.

In addition, we need to consider how to identify and assist persons who have fallen from their desired trajectory and help them develop new qualifications for pursuing the outcomes they desire. If they have acted irresponsibly and are hindered by the residue of their irresponsible behavior and seek to regain momentum, society should assist them in developing the capability for this renewed trajectory. Real opportunity includes promoting capability to renew a trajectory and become qualified for new possibilities if, for example, a person changes their desire to become a welder and seeks to become a lawyer. Structural changes will be needed to enable restored capability. What kind of structural changes might be needed?

It may be as simple as providing persons who have become deficient in hearing with hearing aids or means of communication other than a telephone. It may require a structural change as dramatic as supporting new educational opportunities for a person who seeks to change career paths or for someone emerging from incarceration. In some cases, supportive personal interaction (even forgiveness) may also be needed to fulfill this requirement of fair opportunity. For example, formerly incarcerated persons may need forgiveness from a spouse or their children to gain the social respect necessary to pursue a new trajectory in life. Imagine an incarcerated person who needs forgiveness from a spouse who has been denied material resources because of his corrupt behavior. When he is paralyzed by realizing what he has done and is contrite, forgiveness by a spouse or longtime partner may restore his sense of self-worth. Fair opportunity should not be limited to those who have been treated unfairly. It applies to persons for whom bad luck or even irresponsible behavior has denied capability to seek outcomes that they could have once sought and now desire.[6]

Finally, who should be included? Certainly all, including those freed from incarceration, citizens, and (at least) documented immigrant residents, should receive the equal respect of fair equality of opportunity. Undocumented immigrants trapped in a country should likewise receive all aspects of equal opportunity. Beyond that, what obligation does a nation like the United States have to welcome other immigrants—and which ones—refugees, and asylees? In these cases, the principle does not apply universally, but a nation is obligated by justice to support expanded opportunity for some beyond its borders to advance international justice, even if it is not solely responsible for enforcing international justice.[7]

NOTES

1. John Rawls's most influential publication, *A Theory of Justice*, appeared in 1971. Readers may want to look at the revised edition published in 1999 by Harvard University Press. A brief statement on "fair equality of opportunity" appears on pp. 73–78 of that volume. Readers will note that Rawls neither abandons the concept of merit nor accepts the notion that merit applies only to so-called elite economic positions. It applies to all workplace positions and to civic volunteers and leaders as well. According to Rawls, individuals do not have opportunities absent adequate educational nurturing from society to acquire the merits they desire and need for the positions to which they aspire. I do not think that Rawls's focus on equalizing education goes far enough to assure that society supports individuals and groups to develop qualifications for positions they seek to pursue. While I concur with much of the recent literature critical of meritocracy, I do not abandon merit as a relevant qualification for positions insofar as society supports developing the merit demanded by positions that offer outcomes persons desire.

2. Rawls does not, for example, consider sufficiently what Amartya Sen, Martha Nussbaum, and others—in various writings—say about fostering "capabilities" for persons to qualify for achieving the ends they desire. We should not confuse capability to function in specific ways with actual functioning. To become qualified requires capabilities but also actual functioning. Even if society fosters capabilities, persons are responsible for developing those capabilities to become functionings or qualifications for the outcomes they prefer.

In a recent book, Michael Sandel, a current critic of meritocracy and a critic of John Rawls since the initial publication of *A Theory of Justice*, goes even further than I will by challenging the centrality and even usefulness of a conception of fair equality of opportunity. Sandel seems to ignore efforts to revise and deepen equal opportunity as a widely accepted principle of justice. See *The Tyranny of Merit: What's Become of the Common Good?* (New York: Farrar, Straus, and Giroux, 2020). I will not engage in a comparative critical analysis of either Rawls or Sandel, but readers should know that I have been informed by Sandel but reject his near dismissal of merit, responsibility, qualifications, and equal opportunity. Sandel and Christine Sypnowich share some criticisms of fair equality of opportunity.

At the other end of the spectrum, readers may want to visit a recent book by Adrian Wooldridge, *The Aristocracy of Talent: How Meritocracy Made the Modern World* (New York: Skyhorse Publishing, Inc., 2021). Wooldridge proposes an account of how the rise of merit-based appointments, rooted principally in natural biological differences in intelligence, have advanced both equal economic opportunity and economic efficiency. According to Wooldridge, prior to the development of merit-based opportunities for employment and admissions to universities, outcomes were given unfairly to persons with an established family history or due to nepotistic favoritism. Meritocracy rooted in biological—primarily, cognitive distinction—is, for Woolridge, both just and efficient. In that way, meritocracy "made the modern world." Wooldridge is far too sophisticated to collapse meritocracy and appointments based on qualifications without considering other factors, but he accentuates merit and qualifications based on natural differences of intelligence and justifies unequal—primarily, income—outcomes based on differences of merit alone. He gives little attention to what is needed to develop merit.

My approach, while avoiding a point-by-point statement of differences from Wooldridge, contrasts sharply with his version of merit. I am, however, informed both by Wooldridge's analysis and by my differences from his conception of merit and equal opportunity.

I cite all three of these volumes for purposes of transparency and the possibility that readers will want to explore them. My primary interest is not to offer critical support for my specific conclusions.

3. Younger readers of this book may not know of Ernie Banks. He was an MVP shortstop for the Chicago Cubs and one of my childhood idols in the 1950s. Permit me to introduce him to you for purposes of an illustration that is self-depreciating, amusing, and offers an important illustrative observation.

4. I believe that governments of nations have obligations relevant to opportunities for persons who are not citizens of the nations, but obligations to foreign citizens may differ for various reasons. I will not try to resolve the precise obligations that are owed to residents of other nations. We do have special obligations to undocumented residents in our nation who have no prudent possibilities for life elsewhere.

5. As will become apparent, I shall argue that even individuals responsible for their disability are owed capabilities to overcome those disabilities if and when they are ready for renewed opportunity.

6. Those interested in exploring the literature with contrary views will note that my position on this matter is squarely at odds with Adrian Wooldridge. (See note 2 above.) My position on renewal, especially renewal from a condition attributable to irresponsible behavior, is theologically informed, but arguments paralleling my own are advanced by persons without explicit religious commitments, for example, Michael Sandel on p. 24 of chapter 2.

7. Nicholas Kristof's opinion column on President George W. Bush's support for HIV and AIDS research and therapy comes readily to mind. See "When George W. Bush Was a Hero" in the April 8, 2023, edition of the *New York Times.* According to Kristof, Bush's action has saved as many as twenty-five million lives. Evidently, this policy is in jeopardy because some legislators are concerned that it encourages abortions.

Chapter 2

Opportunity for What? What Is Required and Possible?

NECESSARY INGREDIENTS

With these elements in mind, we can turn to a more fully developed account of what fair equality of opportunity requires and the possibilities for achieving it. We will begin with the freedom to choose desired outcomes.

Freedom to Choose Desired Outcomes

As we have seen, we should not presume the desired outcome of opportunity to be income and wealth. Every citizen should not be presumed to want more income and wealth and a high-profile job or position or status. The degree of inequality or mobility of individuals to achieve outcomes at a higher level than where they started is too often measured by income and social prestige alone. What about persons who want to be police or gather trash for a variety of reasons, ranging from satisfaction with the work and more leisure time to the sense that they will be doing more for the community? What about those who want to work with a community organization with a laudable mission rather than earn more income or prestige? These jobs and the relatively low income for performing them—the income should not be inadequate for a decent life—does not necessarily indicate restricted opportunity. They may reflect freely chosen outcomes.

Studies of the value of education often reveal the implicit assumption that all persons want to be highly paid in prestigious positions. A quick glance at websites on the value of a high school or college education show a significant emphasis—many times, almost exclusive emphasis—on increased earnings resulting from different education levels. This assumption emerges in many rankings of the value of a college education at particular institutions measured by the average cost for the degrees compared to income levels of degree holders at a specified time after graduation. Fortunately, promises of the value of a college degree at particular institutions offer more complex values than lifetime earnings. For example, the website of Carleton College in Northfield, Minnesota, proudly proclaims: "The most important thing our students gain is *how to learn for a lifetime.*" It says that the college cultivates "tools that transform a collection of facts and figures into a way of understanding the world." To the extent that Carleton and other similar schools fulfill these promises, their graduates gain skills such as civic participation and freedom through understanding. Unfortunately, many popular assessments, including some measuring the value of a Carleton College education, still focus predominantly on "career success" and earnings.

Such measurements imply that the value of educational opportunities depends almost exclusively on whether they increase income. With only a little thought, we realize that persons may welcome and pursue educational opportunities for many reasons: discovering what jobs or other positions, for example, parenting or volunteering, bring greater satisfaction or contribute more to the common good. Some persons may wish to hone skills that enable satisfying work, even if it does not offer the highest possible income. They may want to open possibilities for expanded lifelong learning (compare the Carleton College website) or to seek knowledge that leads to better mental and physical health, improvements in their family lives, or better judgments about religious or spiritual life. They may seek more education simply to enhance their understanding of their lives and the world. We should also note that many of these outcomes are not associated narrowly with individual happiness or well-being. They include goals that advance the well-being of others, justice, and the common good. These goals are not antithetical to well-being, but they are not fully described by seeking individual well-being. Many persons gain satisfaction in promoting the good of others as well as society or their community. These consider-ations of the value of education are acutely significant as our nation debates the importance of sustaining a humanities and liberal arts and sciences curriculum.

Martin Luther King Jr. illustrates a departure from the typical self-interested well-being persons seek. His work did not maximize his well-being defined in narrow terms of material gains or physical health, but it did fulfill his desire to advance justice, even if his mis-sion required sacrifices in wealth and personal security. His education at Boston University and the support he received from the Southern Christian Leadership Conference did little to maximize his wealth. However, both provided essential support for his work to advance social justice.

Formal education can be the means to many different ends, and the ends for which persons pursue a variety of kinds and levels of educa-tion differ significantly. We should not presume that a particular kind of education, for example, in the arts or technical skills, is equally desirable for all persons or that the amount of formal education a person achieves indicates greater opportunity. We would be mistaken to conclude that persons with a BS or BA from a reputable four-year institution had greater opportunity or achieved better outcomes. We cannot measure the value of educational opportunity solely by income, advanced degrees, or other specific outcomes. Persons value education for various reasons.

Indeed, some types of education can be ends in themselves—for example, the joy of appreciating good literature or understanding the genetics of the human or some other species. On the other hand, some persons want to study literature as the means to becoming a better teacher or scholar or to learn genetics as the means to becoming a public health official. Some seek to become better artists of a distinctive kind that they envision. Others seek to learn technical skills, such as weld-ing, construction work, or auto mechanics, that enable them to earn an adequate income through satisfying work. The point is that opportunity for education includes expanding persons' choices about what they value in education.

One of my finest former undergraduates married a welder without a college degree. She has worked with nonprofits and in govern-ment. They are both satisfied with their employment and lives and the opportunities they have been offered. We would be mistaken to conclude that she has had more opportunity than her husband or that someone who earns more than she does has had more opportunity.

In addition, not all persons want more education beyond a certain level. Persons may utilize opportunities to pursue ends different from those of us who value higher education or from ends the majority in society aspire to achieve. Some persons value the opportunity for formal education more—and some less—than others.

These different choices about education should not preclude giving others good moral and prudential reasons for more formal education. We may have reasons to persuade particular others that they and society should seek more and a particular kind of formal education for the sake of their goals and well-being or for improving the common good. But equal opportunity should allow, even welcome, them to make choices with which we disagree. Some may pursue technical education for work or for the leisure they prefer over the benefits of a four-year undergraduate education—and certainly over professional and graduate education that may not bring them satisfaction.

Neither more income and wealth nor a particular kind of formal education is conclusive evidence of increased opportunities. These outcomes may not be desired. Other goods may be desired more, which is not to denigrate income or formal education. I contend that some minimal income and education are necessary for any desired outcomes or even to know what outcomes we desire. For some persons, more income and formal education are often desired in some measure for good reasons. However, many persons and groups desire these goods only at a plateau level sufficient for other choices. That level is sufficient for equal opportunity. The fact that some persons choose a moderate plateau in education and income may indicate greater freedom—and opportunity—to pursue desired outcomes.

There may also be good moral arguments for increased formal education or for a broadened humanities and political education that enables responsible civic participation or for an appreciation of the arts that enable enhanced appreciation of culture. I would readily make this moral argument, but these moral arguments should also allow for different choices by others. Some persons believe, perhaps justifiably, that they serve others by focusing on the work or participation in community that satisfies them most. Not all moral conclusions should be subject to legal or even structural coercion. We may laud education that enhances culture, broad experience, or political participation without deploying structures that nearly coerce persons to aspire to this level and type of education. Fair opportunity incorporates the right to moral disagreements and different moral conclusions without forfeiting persistence in making moral claims and giving reasons for them.

These observations about opportunity as choice for levels and kinds of income, wealth, and education—and even different moral conclusions about the desirability of more of these and other outcomes—apply to myriad other ends persons may seek: the amount and kinds of work that contribute to the economy and the common good and the amount of work in relation to leisure time and what to do with that leisure. Consider health and the reasons for seeking health, the kind and extent of family life, or leadership and its contributions to the community. Some persons and families may prefer less demanding jobs that contribute directly to a community and do not dictate investments of huge amounts of time. I could go on. In sum, a society that values persons', families', and associations' freedom to pursue different goals and visions of well-being nurtures opportunities with latitude for multiple ends. It eschews efforts to measure levels of opportunity by specific outcomes achieved.

Freedom to Change Desired Outcomes

Such a society also offers flexibility for persons and associations to change the ends for which they strive. Someone who begins an education for a job seeking primarily income may evolve to realize that other goals are preferable. Think of high-level lawyers or financiers who decide to become ministers or rabbis or leaders of civic organizations. Imagine paralegal employees or healthcare workers who later want to pursue education in the law or professional medicine. Others who eschew higher education as a young person may decide later to continue through undergraduate and graduate school. Elderly persons may wish to pursue formal education for its intrinsic value. Opportunities for varied outcomes are relevant throughout life, not merely at some starting line.

Although popular opinion commonly associates equal opportunity with an equal starting line, the view of fair equality of opportunity proposed here strives to provide necessary means for the freedom of persons to change the varied outcomes they pursue. That requires fostering capabilities to change outcomes sought throughout life. To be sure, the role of structural support for developing capabilities for new outcomes may vary—for example, society does not have the same obligation to support education for elderly persons indulging in self-satisfying education as it does to enable a young paralegal to undertake a legal education. Nevertheless, society should not encumber developing capabilities and, in many cases, should facilitate new capabilities for new opportunities.

Changes in the outcomes opportunity offers include changes in judgments about what persons value as well as changing capabilities as we age. As we grow older, capabilities for different outcomes inevitably change. Fair opportunity necessarily differs for a sixteen-year-old, a middle-aged person, a recent retiree, and a person over one hundred. While society should not be expected to fund entirely a new formal education for elderly persons, elderly persons are likely to desire continued learning and social interactions and even more formal education or employment. Persons' desired outcomes change. The freedom to pursue those new outcomes will require fostering new capabilities. Aging persons should be free to choose from among a variety of outcomes they wish to achieve and can pursue without great cost to others. Families have a role here in providing for their aging members, but so do social institutions and government through supporting stimulating social interaction, even among those suffering from memory and language loss, and ways in which older persons can volunteer in their communities. Provision for fair equality of opportunity must adjust to the realities of age and other differences, for example, health capacities, that occur throughout life.

Opportunity, understood in this way, is measured by the freedom to pursue goods and positions for different ends and quantities of an outcome. It also respects freedom to change those desired ends over time, whether due to changes in judgment, health events, family, or the necessary realities of aging. Consequently, we are mistaken to assume fixed values, goals, or conceptions of well-being by which to measure success in offering fair equality opportunity. Imagine a sixty-year-old widower who longs for the opportunity to become involved in the education of his young children. Opportunity, rightly understood, enables persons, families, and other associations to pursue different ends and to revise their ends over time.

Moral Advice and Changing Desired Outcomes

Moreover, these changes may include noncoercive advice from others. As alluded to earlier, freedom for individuals or groups to change their goals does not preclude moral and prudential advice short of coercive laws and structures. We may want to encourage individuals, families, or associated groups to pursue an educational trajectory to advance their own well-being or a public good like health or advancing social justice without precluding their freedom to choose among opportunities available to them. We should not confuse moral discussion and disagreement with coercive measures to dictate choice and force new outcomes.

Our current debates about abortion practices may be the most vivid matter in which we fail to distinguish moral criticism from legal coercion. We could have more open discussion and even agreement about abortion without legally coercing pregnant and potentially pregnant women. Moral advice does not entail stipulating acceptable outcomes for a pregnancy. Moral judgments and advice should not be confused with legal enforcement. We can view abortion as a moral issue subject to open moral discussion and disagreement while protecting the legal and structural freedom of pregnant women to decide in consultation with others. They are by far in the best position to judge the dramatic consequences and outcomes, especially for their lives but also for the lives of family members, friends, and the children for which they are or may in the future be responsible. These considerations include the consequences for a fetus. This view differs markedly from claiming that pregnant women are free to decide what to do with their own bodies without regard to moral criticism from family members and close associates. Persons in reasoned and respectful discourse can disagree about the morality of abortion while ensuring the legal freedom for pregnant woman to decide. There may currently be no more momentous issue regarding the distinct roles of moral and legal elements in facilitating the outcomes of lives.

If a decision about consequences and outcomes as dramatic as abortion can be subject to moral discourse, surely freedom regarding matters of education, income prospects, leisure time, community participation, and so forth can incorporate moral discourse while respecting the freedom to change individual and group ends. The choice is not between individuals deciding their preferred outcomes without consultation and legal enforcement of outcomes persons must pursue.

Structures that offer freedom for different choices do not preclude strong but respectful advice, prudential and moral, that recommends a change in inchoately formed decisions while refraining from legal restraints on persons' freedoms. This may include admonition to correct irresponsible behavior and the means to change it. In short, opportunities to renew or change directions in goals include engaging in discourse that engenders thoughtful consideration of options.

Means to Choose and Qualify for Desired Outcomes

As briefly noted earlier, equalizing opportunity for freedom to choose entails providing the means required for the outcomes persons seek. Without access to the necessary means to pursue chosen ends, opportunity is limited and choices of what to seek are no more than wishes or dreams. There is no freedom when there are severely limited possibilities even for choosing ends and for the means to obtain the knowledge and skills to achieve desired outcomes, especially for changing ends and enabling new possibilities. Ensuring that an impoverished person or a woman can be accepted in a new position without regard to her previous income or gender does not assure her the opportunity for that position. She also needs help to become qualified.

For example, a woman who seeks a modest income using technical skills, with adequate resources for a family life and the leisure to fish and knit for her family, will need a relevant education and the health to enjoy these things. She will need a legal structure that supports this family arrangement, available adequate housing in neighborhoods safe for her family, and an environment in which fish thrive and fishing is permitted and possible. Access to an appropriate education and health are necessary means, even if the highest level of either education or health does not have the highest priority for this person. If a couple of the same gender seeks a legally binding agreement for their relationship, they will need laws and technology that protect a stable and respected family life and that provide means for children, if desired.

In the first case, society will need to protect the environment for fish and offer freedom and regulation to both allow for and sustain the prospect of fishing. In the second case, society will need to provide the legal and technological means for a same-sex marriage with children. The point is that supporting opportunity requires much more than individual freedom to engage in market exchanges and much more than job offers without discrimination based on prejudices irrelevant to performance. Fair opportunity requires societal action enabling individuals first to freely choose and then to pursue chosen goals and well-being.

As implied earlier, individual opportunities for the freedom and capability to seek varied outcomes also require collaborative support from families and associations. Families and groups can, of course, exploit individuals and restrict opportunities. Sometimes highly isolated religious or civic associations restrict persons' minimal education or participation in social structures for funding basic needs. Some religious groups reject the value of basic education for their children or eschew participation in societal arrangements for basic healthcare or pensions for elderly persons. Some family members violently, or at least coercively, try to restrict legitimate freedoms of other family members.

In these cases, societal structures must regulate families and associations to ensure that they do not limit individual opportunities, but these interpersonal collaborative arrangements, that is, civic associations and families, also enable distinctive opportunities. Isolated individuals, even supported by legal structures, cannot enable some opportunities. Assuming that opportunity can emerge from individuals supported by structures and regulations alone imprudently ignores that desired outcomes are rarely possible unless individuals are part of collaborative groups such as families and religious and civic organizations. Children and spouses, for example, need support from families and small groups to foster opportunities to choose and achieve new possibilities or to recover from a period of irresponsible behavior. Individual choices and endeavors, even supported by societal structures, are insufficient for real opportunity. Families and religious and civic groups are necessary, in addition to a willing individual and societal legal support, to pursue distinctive ends such as highly environmentally friendly agriculture. I have in mind a family in my community that unites to raise and sell flowers and food an individual alone could not hope to achieve. Their operation is an operation of a nuclear and extended family and depends on their collaboration with local markets.

Freedom to choose and pursue outcomes also requires a social structure of course. Governments and unified civic institutions enhance and foster the limited capacities of individuals by nurturing capabilities for new outcomes. I distinguish capacities and capabilities throughout this book, using capability as a power for freedom of choice and functioning that societies can foster and capacity as a given power that cannot always, or easily, be altered by individuals and groups. Building on capacities requires society to nurture capabilities to function and become qualified for opportunities. If my limited capacities for memory or eyesight are irremediable, my capabilities in these areas cannot be enhanced. On the other hand, most capacities can be revised or enhanced by education, therapy, or altered circumstances so persons may function at a different level. I could not have developed the skills of my childhood idol, Ernie Banks, and my family and the groups that supported me in my local community could not have developed my academic qualifications. Still, a university system and other educational institutions supported by government enabled me to slowly develop the qualifications to become a college professor. Social structures can foster new capabilities and greater freedom for choosing and pursuing outcomes.

The distinction between capacities and capabilities may change over time. For example, a society may learn to adjust circumstances so that persons who could not function in a particular position can do so, or it may develop new remedies for health problems like HIV/AIDS or dementia. In these instances, capacities may be changed. Even if they remain limiting, we can foster capabilities that expand opportunities. For example, we may not be able to eradicate all limiting capacities associated with HIV/AIDS or dementia, but we can develop therapies and change conditions for outcomes that enable persons with these limiting capacities to expand their capabilities for choices and achievements. For example, a person with dementia may be enabled to expand interpersonal interactions in a highly structured community setting.

We cannot deny that limited capacities restrict some capabilities and freedoms, but society can do a great deal to build on capacities to render them capabilities for greater freedom to function in pursuing new outcomes.

Means to Recover from Vestiges of Misfortune

In addition, I claim that persons should also have the means to recover from difficulties in life, whether caused by injustices that disadvantage the victim, by bad fortune (e.g., a mental health problem or unanticipated disability related to a desired outcome), or even irresponsible behavior (e.g., an addiction that the person might have avoided, bad habits, a period of slough, or illicit actions and just incarceration). Opportunity must expand possibilities foreclosed by the vestiges of these disruptions, whether self-inflicted, caused by misfortune or injustices to a victim, or, most likely, a combination of these. Difficulty, as understood here, is not merely an isolated failure to achieve a desired outcome. In that case, one could prepare and try again. The difficulty here is an event or course of events that hinder the means to choose and pursue new outcomes—for example, a medium-term physical or psychological inability to envision and pursue desired outcomes.

For example, a contrite person ravaged by guilt for wrongdoing may need institutional and personal forgiveness to effectively pursue new ends. Christians may be reminded of the Prodigal Son in the gospel of Luke. A criminal justice system that permanently undermines the social bases of self-respect stands in the way of these new possibilities in life. Note again that fair opportunity is not limited to respecting individual qualifications for a particular position. It requires various kinds of societal support and sometimes interpersonal support for overcoming disruptions in a person's capabilities to effect new outcomes. It requires positive action, not merely refraining from unjust discrimination in appointments to positions.

Individual effort alone cannot easily overcome these impediments to choosing new outcomes and developing qualifications, whether they are the consequences of injustice, chance, or irresponsibility that a person later regrets and for which he is contrite. He needs to be granted the privilege that others have received from a just society, the good fortune of innate talents, by nurturing from others, or by "second chances" granted by society or other persons.

Philosophical literature often calls for expanding possibilities, including for persons with disabilities, for making choices and implementing them. Amartya Sen and Martha Nussbaum are well-known for advocating fostering capabilities to expand "real opportunity." Philosophical literature frequently advocates a form of reparation that grants new opportunities to those who have been harmed by injustice. Disruptions caused by misfortune and even more by the wrongdoing of a citizen are another matter. Philosophers rarely account for renewing capabilities that have been lost by misfortune and almost never comment on the need to enable persons who have been psychologically debilitated due to culpable actions and ensuing guilt. It is all too common to attribute these misfortunes to just consequences that do not need to be remedied. This rarity may be due to reluctance to utilize comprehensive moral conceptions associated with religious traditions in a pluralistic society. Religious traditions have certainly played a role in illuminating how conceptions of grace, redemption, and forgiveness inform justice and thereby equal opportunity. The Prodigal Son needed his father's forgiveness to reconcile with his family and community. I maintain, however, that versions of these conceptions are rational and persuasive independent of the comprehensive religious doctrines with which they are sometimes associated.[1]

Michael Sandel, a Harvard philosopher (not a theologian), confirms this claim for rational support for assertions that terms like "grace" and "forgiveness" can be justified outside the religious context. Sandel writes that the "contingency of our lot" associated with the "grace of God," "accident of birth," or "mystery of fate" (used interchangeably by Sandel) reminds us of the distinctive privileges that constitute part of our opportunities that others may not enjoy. Language such as "grace" is amenable to and can be persuasive to persons unassociated with a particular religious tradition, even as rich religious traditions help us appreciate these phenomena that secular traditions often fail to imagine.[2]

Conclusions

In sum, fair opportunity should not be measured by and should not be locked into income and wealth or, for that matter, into any other particular outcome. Opportunity permits different persons or unified and internally just collaborative groups, such as a family, to nurture and seek different amounts and types of these goods. All persons and groups want some income, but they may prefer competing goods such as leisure or low-wage or nonpaying civic action to more income. All want some education, but they may not prefer sixteen years to obtain a bachelor's degree or more focusing on technical skills—or on literature and the arts.

At the same time, fair opportunity requires some earnings, education, health, and so forth to have the means to pursue whatever goals and conception of well-being persons prefer. Income, although necessary at some level, is neither the sole end of opportunity nor the sole or always the most effective means to pursue the ends persons choose. Some income, education, health, and other goods are necessary means for freely choosing and pursuing ends. A simple life in community with others requires some steady income, basic education, and decent provision for good health. I will discuss below the extent to which the United States fails to provide each of these minimally basic capabilities.

This freedom for individuals and groups to pursue different outcomes, including conceptions of well-being, allows for moral criticism and discussion because not all criticism of a course of action calls for coercion and legal restrictions. We shall see that individual freedom of opportunity is at some point limited, but the freedom in opportunity requires individual and group latitude in choosing outcomes that prohibit legal resolution of all differences.

Moreover, fair opportunity requires that these means to choose ends are available at different times and are not foreclosed by actions or inaction at anyone point in time. Persons must be able to change their preferences for well-being or to renew possibilities when disruptions occur, even if the disruptions are largely self-inflicted by irresponsible behavior. For this reason, the bromide that all should have an equal starting point is grossly incomplete. Opportunity also requires real possibilities for changing life goals and lifestyle.

These opportunities do not exist without a structure to support them. The structure must go well beyond freedom for legal interpersonal transactions based on given preferences and qualifications alone. Many philosophers, including John Rawls, call this broader framework a "basic structure." The basic structure must be constituted by institutions (legal, governmental, civic, economic) that enable persons to pursue goods such as income, education, health, and more. All opportunities require educational and healthcare institutions and some means for food and modest recreation.

We will explore different judgments regarding what constitutes a just basic structure and whether individual actions in addition to the basic structure are required to ensure maximum fair quality of opportunity. Freedom for individual interaction without discrimination based on prejudices extraneous to qualifications is necessary but grossly insufficient to provide the means for fair opportunity.

To illustrate this rather abstract assertion once again: Fair opportunity for you requires more than others' respecting your qualifications. It also requires that society provide the means you need—for example, an education, health, legal arrangements for a family, or an environment—for you to become qualified. You cannot create these conditions individually, no matter how responsible you may be in pursuing opportunities. Without these means, you have little freedom to pursue—or even freely and realistically choose—the ends you desire. You cannot become qualified on your own. A "basic structure" to foster capability that exceeds our given capacities to become qualified is a necessary means. Even some forms of personal interaction are required—for example, encouragement and respect from a colleague or forgiveness from a spouse or parent.

WHAT NECESSARY MEANS?

Before exploring the policies, practices, and actions fair equality opportunity requires, let's identify with greater specificity the means required for the freedom to choose and for persons to pursue the many legitimate values and ends citizens seek at different times in their lives. A variety of recent proposals go beyond avoiding discrimination based on factors extraneous to qualifications.

Beyond Opportunities Given at Birth

As noted, John Rawls's well-known conception of fair equal opportunity stipulated that opportunity requires that society compensate for social circumstances of birth and location that hinder education as a means to acquire qualifications. In doing so, Rawls takes a step in justifying the obligation to foster qualifications as well as distinguishing this fostering from mere prejudicial favoritism. Others go well beyond Rawls's modest modification of "positions open to the most qualified."

All of us are familiar with calls for affirmative action or even a form of reparations for members of some groups to compensate for the harms caused by previous unjust discrimination by law or by implicit racial or other kinds of bias in awarding positions—for example, admission to educational institutions. Rawls does not reject compensatory action for previous wrongs. He avoids that issue by proposing ideal principles rather than remedies, for example, affirmative action, for previous noncompliance. Like many others who have written about justice, I will argue that fair equality of opportunity requires more than principles for an ideal society. It requires that we redress the realities of current unjust structures and the residues of previous injustices. This compensatory justice considers how to correct unjust structures, for example, an unfair policing and criminal justice system, and not merely how to provide for ideal policing or criminal justice. This approach requires use of social sciences to determine how and when the unjust structures undermine fair opportunity and, then, remedy the unfairness.

There are, for example, proposals to introduce greater justice into the structure of opportunity. They include assured access to quality healthcare and addressing underlying health disparities due to inadequate healthcare and poor public health, which have unequal consequences for different groups. For example, some groups of working-class persons must ride public transportation and work in tight quarters exposed to infections. These persons, disproportionately African Americans, are more susceptible to infections from diseases such as COVID-19. This shortcoming includes concern for injustices in the criminal justice system—policing, trials, incarceration, and restoration to full citizenship following incarceration—that undermine the security of some racial minorities and impoverished citizens, males in particular.

One philosopher argues that a full set of "resources" could provide the necessary means to achieve fair opportunity. Some claim that inequality of political power, often associated with significant economic disparity, undermines efforts to enhance the means for vulnerable persons to pursue the ends, goals, and well-being they choose. No one, not even Christine Sypnowich (see chapter 1, note 1) argues that fulfilling a rigid particular conception of well-being is necessary, but two important philosophers have argued that six core elements of well-being are required.[3]

Each of these terms seeks to describe necessary means for valued ends that persons desire and cannot achieve by their own will and effort alone. Help from society is necessary. In sum, there is less than fair opportunity for persons who are not granted these supports. Martha Nussbaum and Amartya Sen are well-known for proposing equality of "capability" for persons of unequal innate capacities or fortune so that they can develop "functionings" required for varied goals or well-being that persons may choose. This capability is necessary for persons to have the freedom to achieve their own goals and well-being—and even to envision the choices they desire. Sen has written explicitly about the difference between capability—for many different functionings—and human capital, which targets economic ends alone. Neither income and wealth, human capital, nor other resources alone assure the capability to develop qualifications or assure the possibility to develop functionings needed to make choices about what constitutes well-being and to purse a preferred conception of well-being.[4]

The proposal developed in this book follows a variation of this idea of basic or equal capability. (Equal capability is the ideal. Basic capability is almost always possible, even if it is not equal in some cases.) Capability as opportunity not only goes beyond opportunity as being judged on one's qualifications; it also exceeds adjustments for unfortunate social circumstances (Rawls) or access to a designated set of resources (Dworkin). It considers "real opportunity" (Amartya Sen's terminology) as the capability to be and act as one chooses unencumbered by fortune determined by either individuals' natural or social characteristics. For example, a person whose speech is limited by mild autism can be enabled to talk and interact normally by corrective measures provided by speech and other forms of therapy. Persons encumbered by mental health issues can often be restored to healthy functioning by effective therapy. In these instances, fostering capability transforms and enhances natural capacities, at least in a limited way.

The notion that natural characteristics, either innate or acquired by happenstance, should not limit opportunities is distinctive but not unique to Sen and Nussbaum. Think about a person whose options are severely limited by physical, psychological, or mental capacities at birth or incurred by misfortune—or even by failures of her own making. Does she currently have an opportunity to be or do what she wants? She may not even have an opportunity to envision, let alone pursue, what she wants to become. Of course, not all natural or irreversible bad fortune can be undone or even drastically altered, but specific individual natural and social circumstances can often be adjusted to expand the capability a person has to pursue ends of their choosing. Furthermore, capabilities can be expanded by changing what persons are required to do to function effectively in positions. For example, we can make alternative arrangements to communicate for those who have no use of their fingers or for those for whom direct personal conversation is a challenge. Capabilities enabled and limited by individual characteristics of natural and social fortune can be revised and expanded by societal actions.

To avoid being overwhelmed by abstract distinctions, let's consider more possibilities. Limitations due to dyslexia or Asperger's or Down syndrome can be altered by therapy. They can also be altered without changes intrinsic to the individual by changing the circumstances of a workplace, an educational setting, a recreational option, and so on. The capability of older persons with dementia can be expanded by changes in their surroundings and the circumstances of social interaction. We are now seeing stories, especially beyond the United States, of communities of persons with dementia, interspersed with some medical persons and therapists, that offer key internal grocery shops, pubs, and theaters. Opportunities for functioning can sometimes be expanded by the tone and respect conveyed in interactions. The way in which we voice expectations for a person can enhance their capabilities by engendering self-respect.

I have in mind a grocery clerk in my town, afflicted by autism or a related mental or social disability. His meaningful functioning at work and in civic affairs (reciting long poems, for example) has been forged by tailoring the workplace and civic possibilities to his considerable special skills. He is respected and bolstered by many of his professional colleagues and fellow citizens. Note that increasing resources fails to account for some of these enhancements of capability. This young man needs respect, encouragement, and an appropriate setting for his possibilities more than he needs additional resources.

These affirming expectations are sometimes encompassed by structures that lead to a position and are sometimes expressed in interpersonal exchanges. Sometimes social structures shape cultural habits that undergird confidence and self-respect—for example, when laws require accommodating the workplace to fit the qualities of a disabled person.

Sometimes individual or association decisions revise social structures and cultural habits—for example, when a person or group suggests a means for a person with specific talents to display those talents in an unusual manner. Memorizing and reciting a long poem he could not read is one such means for a person with autism. Changing laws and policies, as suggested above, are more coercive in shaping our individual behaviors toward others. Suggesting that a person memorize and recite a poem he could not read depends more on independent choices that depart from both a structure and an imbued culture. These individual actions also shape a noncoercive structural change and revise cultural expectations. Think of how we are taught by example not to focus on eccentricities of physical appearance in a workplace setting.[5]

Workplaces and educational and recreational settings can also be changed to expand options for persons with supposedly debilitating physical limitations. This particular expansion of capabilities has become more pronounced recently. My first experience was as an undergraduate at the University of Illinois in Champaign-Urbana in the early 1960s. The university proudly (and boastfully!) provided bus service throughout the large campus for persons who could neither walk nor climb the steps of a bus. At the time, the university made much—perhaps so much that it made persons feel inferior—of what was a distinctive provision to expand opportunities for a large group of persons on a campus. Memory and youthful naivety at the time prevent me from recalling how extensive other adjustments—say, in the classroom—were, but it is easy to imagine the changes in opportunities for higher education on a large campus. These changes were not at the time legally required.

We have also discovered how to expand opportunities for persons with an established sexual orientation without altering the orientation. Limitations to family life based on a given sexual orientation can be revised by legal, cultural, and individual behavior so that lesbian, gay, and transgendered persons can marry, form families, and raise children with both structural and interpersonal support. Individual changes for medical practice and ethics also have a role in this context, but structurally induced cultural changes for expanding capability are significant.

We have not been broadly successful in ending racially segregated housing and schools. Perhaps we thought that we had settled structural causes of Black/White racial segregation with court and legislative policy changes in the fifties and sixties and assumed that residual segregation resulted from individual choices by Blacks and Whites, some of them benign as they pertain to equal opportunity. Recent scholarship has challenged that view. Empirical evidence shows that de jure segregation during the Jim Crow era remains due to tax policy, zoning laws, and the failure to counteract structural forces that contribute to racial segregation in both housing and education. This empirical evidence does not prove inveterate systematic racism or that a general theory or ideology explains segregation or racism. It nonetheless raises specific questions about legal and structural issues that contribute to persistent segregation and unequal opportunities. Structural, legally enforced or countenanced, factors continue to hinder opportunity even in the absence of comprehensive systematic legal segregation. The issue cannot be resolved by assertions for or against critical race theory. These legal factors, however, establish that continuing segregation is not merely de facto issuing from individual choices. Laws and structures remain barriers to racial fair opportunity in this realm. The problem includes, but goes beyond, individual choices by White or Black persons, families, and associations.[6]

Policies bearing on elderly persons offer yet another example of structural and interpersonal behavior interacting to secure fair equality of opportunity. It is a biological fact that elderly persons have a lower capacity for stamina, memory, focus, and other capabilities, but changes in public health, medicine, and arrangements for family and civic life can renew much of their capability. These structural arrangements demolished stereotypes of elderly persons. They demonstrate that augmented capabilities can mitigate perceived biological limitations. They are not inalterable. Changing personal attitudes are insufficient to expand capabilities, but they are contributory and may also be necessary. Many older persons need the social respect that occurs when others of various ages recognize older persons' special skills.

More illustrations are possible. These vividly demonstrate that both structural factors and interpersonal behavior bear on fair opportunity. They also illustrate that neither human nature nor the combination of human nature and cultural expectations is a given that forecloses expanding capability to function and achieve goals. Opportunity does not have to be arbitrarily limited by facts of human nature, whether innate or acquired. Changing technology and cultural attitudes enable efforts to expand what persons are capable of doing and becoming.

Specifying and Effecting Necessary Means

The concept of equal or even basic capability lacks the specificity that we understandably desire. There are good reasons for this lack of specificity. Even though human nature is malleable in interaction with different environments so that nature does not dictate capability, nature and established capabilities are not entirely plastic. Capability can never be molded to produce identical (or even equal) capability for every outcome. Furthermore, equal capability, where achievable, cannot be linked to specific goods or functioning outcomes that all can seek according to their choices. There are limits to fostering identical and even equal capabilities for functioning.

Two sets of reasons inform this observation: (1) the impossibility of securing identical capability for all outcomes and (2) the importance of preserving freedom to choose what constitutes individual well-being as well as retaining personal responsibility to execute opportunity.

Self-Identity

First, although human nature and firmly established traits of a person are not inalterable, they are not infinitely malleable. Certainly, matters such as education, healthcare, and other factors can be changed in ways that expand the established capabilities of persons. Nevertheless, intrinsic characteristics formed by innate nature and established identity are distinctive. These characteristics establish necessary and different beginning points that limit and channel any expansion of capability for persons. Consider largely established mental, physical, or psychological capacities or individual aspects of health, for example, skin vulnerable to intense ultraviolet rays. It is not surprising, although I will argue ultimately mistaken, that John Rawls and others contend that fair equality of opportunity requires adjustment of social circumstances while accepting attributes of human nature as givens.

Rawls and others view natural characteristics as givens, although Rawls famously mitigates his reliance of the givenness of human nature by arguing that the fruits of these natural attributes should be distributed to benefit all members of society. On this view, justice requires those blessed by nature to utilize those blessings to benefit others. My childhood idol, Ernie Banks, should share is baseball prowess with fans, and a person who has special talents as a surgeon should benefit the rest of us with her special skills. She should not expect to gain whatever is possible in the marketplace by getting as much income and prestige as possible via her rare ability.

Rawls did not consider those naturally advantaged more meritorious than others. They do nothing to deserve the natural talents. Hence, he held that the benefits of these naturally given talents should be distributed as equally as possible consistent with freedom, that is, no outright coercion. He allowed for inequality of outcomes consistent with market freedoms and efficiencies but only insofar as the unequal outcomes are needed for the benefit of others. Thus we will reward the aforementioned surgeon to use her skills to benefit all of us, especially the least well-off among us, only to the extent that is necessary to persuade her to hone and use her skills for others. In this arrangement, the unequal outcomes are incentives that benefit others, especially the least advantaged.

Society may deploy taxes, subsidies, and regulations to limit the rewards of these naturally skilled persons. We may use taxes and subsidies for healthcare for the patients of our surgeon just as long as we do not coerce her to deploy her skills as a surgeon. Justice requires taxes on persons like her to support the health of her patients or the education of those less naturally blessed. She does not merit whatever she can command in an unfettered market. Her unequal share of income is justified only insofar as it is necessary to persuade her to offer her special abilities. The same principle applies to an artist. What do we need to offer him to bless us with his work? In some cases, as with the artist and a renowned baseball player, part of the unequal reward is special attention and accolades that may be as or more important than income.

Some advocates for meritocracy—Adrian Wooldridge is exemplary—believe natural talents indicate merit that should be rewarded fully in the marketplace. Rawls and others contend that methods that mobilize natural talent for the equal benefit of all are consistent with and even demanded by equal opportunity. Unlike Rawls, Wooldridge contends that merit rooted in natural inequalities deserves unmitigated recognition. In this case, no adjustment in distribution—whether for income or other desirable outcomes—is warranted due to lack of "merit" associated with natural advantages. The naturally talented deserve what they can get.

Rawls was famous for his "difference principle," which limited unequal rewards to the naturally advantaged to inequalities necessary to benefit all persons, especially the least advantaged. This principle of justice limits inequalities of income and other outcomes to those necessary to incentivize the naturally talented to benefit the least well-off persons in society. In other words, persons and groups may justly receive beneficial outcomes from their natural advantages only insofar as their unequal outcomes benefit those with fewer natural advantages. For another example, society should be willing to compensate highly skilled lawyers more if it is necessary to induce them to benefit clients with fewer natural advantages.

These natural characteristics are viewed by many (Rawls among them) as givens, even though the fruits of these innate natural attributes are distributed to benefit all members of society rather than awarded based on supposed natural merits. Natural talents do not merit special rewards. No one has earned the rewards. Rawls, unlike those who approve of inequalities obtained in an unfettered market, did not view persons with natural talents as meriting higher income. They do nothing to deserve higher income or other privileges, though Rawls unfortunately focused almost exclusively on income outcomes.

Readers do not have to understand fully Rawls's difference principle to see the importance of this dispute for our considered views of equal opportunity and justice. Rawls's views continue to articulate important opposition to the view that innately blessed members of society merit greater outcomes. They also fall short of the view of others of us that innate capacities can be made more equal by fostering capabilities that enable the less innately blessed to choose and pursue outcomes beyond what the innate capacities permit.

Rawls and others have, correctly in my judgment, argued that persons with greater innate talents should not receive higher incomes unless the income (or other incentivizing inequalities) is necessary to induce the maximum possible benefit to the least well-off persons, that is, those with more modest natural talents but no less deserving. On this view, highly sophisticated athletes might receive more income as well as public recognition not because they deserve it, but because it induces them to deploy their innate talents in a way that benefits less-talented members of society.[7] Note that naturally unequal talents are, for Rawls, still givens that cannot be equalized. (I demur from the view that they are absolute givens. Fostering capabilities for functioning can expand innate capacities. I concur that whatever special talents we are given should be shared with others.) For Rawls, benefits from these given talents can be justly equalized to the extent that tax policy, subsidies, and regulations within a market still enable choice in preparation for and execution of professions.

As indicated, this is not an acceptable end of the story. This book follows research in child development and other areas of human behavior that demonstrate conclusively that nature and nurture or environmental factors are not in competition for determining human functioning but always interacting. The interaction, not nature or nurture separately, fosters capabilities for functioning.[8] For example, we have learned that childhood stimulation in the family and in institutional settings fosters capabilities that nature does not provide and compensates for some natural deficits. However, recognizing a variety of integrated possibilities between nature and nurture accounts for the reality that human capability at various points becomes alterable in only limited ways.

For example, since I was born with defective vision that could not at the time be corrected sufficiently for me to hit a pitched baseball, nothing could have been done—at least at the time—that would offer me the freedom to become a professional baseball player. That did not preclude a societal structure that permitted me an education to become a college teacher. My given capacities also allowed me to appreciate the talents of professional baseball players, especially Ernie Banks of the Chicago Cubs. My opportunities were different from but arguably roughly equal to Ernie Banks, even if I fell short of achieving at his level. (I hasten to add that our currently unjust society does not enable such relatively equal capabilities to function.) In sum, differences in established and virtually unalterable attributes do not permit identical capabilities to achieve at any endeavor we choose, even though capabilities of roughly equal value are often possible.

Ernie Banks and Henry Louis Gates Jr. may have been granted roughly equal capabilities and achieved roughly equally valuable outcomes, but they did not have identical capabilities for whatever endeavor they chose. It is unlikely that Henry Louis Gates Jr. could have been a Major League MVP even if he desired that outcome; and

as much as I admired some of Ernie Banks's public pronouncements—
for example, "Let's play three"—I doubt he could have influenced our
societal views on race and justice in the way that Gates has.[9]

We must concede that within these possibilities for different and
enhanced capabilities, unequal natural or established talents persist
and that inequalities of outcomes flow from them. While different
capabilities may sometimes be equally valuable, they are rarely the
same. No intervention could have given me the capability to hit a baseball like Ernie Banks. We do not have to accept Rawls's and others'
sharp distinction between malleable social circumstances that can be
largely equalized and human nature as an inalterable given to recognize limitations in altering established differences in individual human
possibilities.

There are social and psychological, as well as natural, limits to
developing or reshaping capabilities. Even if technology and structural policies and practices to develop fully identical capability by
revising natural or socially established characteristics were possible,
at some point persons changed by structural policies would not retain
a personal identity or self-ownership. We would not be developing
the equal capability for a self but for some remade and different self.
Our self-identity is shaped by an interaction between nature and the
circumstances in which we develop. I, for example, am a White male
(by gender as well as biologically) with damaged eyesight who lived
and worked on a Midwestern farm through high school. At what point
does changing each of these traits in order to augment capability so that
I could be just like Ernie Banks or Robert Louis Gates Jr. deprive me
of self-ownership? Efforts to give me identical capability with others
would at some point deny me self-identity and self-respect rather than
expanding my opportunities.

In sum, equal capability is not identical capability for any position
individuals choose to pursue. Adjustments to innate or established
human nature in interaction with what becomes recalcitrant social circumstances to create totally different capabilities—supposing it were
possible—would obviate a given self-identity. We would no longer be
the same person.

Freedom and Responsibility

Second, some critics of capability as a standard for opportunity do not believe that it goes far enough in identifying equal outcomes as a measure for achieving the standard for equal opportunity. They turn to common or even the same goods as necessary steps to well-being. For example, persons should have the same understanding and level of health. Or they should develop identifiable functions (such as financial analysis or artistic achievement) to achieve just opportunities for all.

This is tricky territory. Some level of common good such as income, security, or shelter; some level of education and understanding and health; and some level of functioning for financial analysis or aesthetic achievement are all required to be capable of choosing and achieving ends. We need some education and health to choose how much and what kind of education and health we wish to pursue and some level of income and security to live and choose to seek more income and security. We need some level of financial and aesthetic functioning to know how and how much we value them.

Still, two problems undermine measuring these goods and functions by specific outcomes required for equality of opportunity: (1) our *freedom* to value and seek different kinds or amounts of education, health, financial wizardry, artistry, or even security and (2) our *responsibility* to exercise our opportunity for these outcomes in order to achieve them.

As discussed earlier, some individuals may want less education so that they have more time for other endeavors or to pursue leisure. They may also prefer different kinds of education. Some prefer technical knowledge or science; others prefer the humanities or arts. They certainly do not all want the same kind of education. As pertains to health, some may prefer a more sedentary life that somewhat jeopardizes health. Some may choose the pleasures of eating amounts and kinds of food that do not maximize health outcomes. Measuring opportunity by whether persons have the same educational or health outcomes precludes the freedom for fair opportunities for these different ends.

I hasten to reiterate that we may want to make prudential or even moral arguments for exercise, healthy eating, or advanced and specialized education—and many other practices. The argument may even include how such practices benefit the common good. We may still avoid any legal or structural coercion to demand these practices. Once again, not all moral views we defend entail coercive enforcement.

Justice requires persons have freedom to choose the outcomes they wish to pursue except when that freedom forecloses others' opportunities and rights.

Insisting on identical outcomes as a measure of equal capability also precludes being responsible for the outcomes one prefers. An individual may squander opportunities for health or the capability for the artistry he claims to desire. We have rejected the view that individual merit alone constitutes the qualifications for a position or appointment, but that does not preclude a more qualified understanding of merit as taking responsibility for achievement when capability has been granted. Individual responsibility is necessary even when merit is not solely attributable to individual effort.[10] Expecting responsible behavior of persons to pursue the outcomes they choose continues to have a role to incentivize individuals and benefit society. The expectation motivates desired behavior and benefits the common good without denying the need for equal capability and opportunity.

Retaining individual freedom and responsibility precludes measuring equal opportunity as specifying enforcement of a kind or quantity of education, health, security, housing, artistic or financial achievement, or any other good or functioning level.

If society invests disproportionately in education or financial or artistic programs that many individuals do not desire, the structure becomes coercive in subsidizing goods or activities that some persons do not choose. It denies the opportunity to choose among different outcomes.

Securing outcomes also requires individual responsibility for exercising one's capabilities. Supplying outcomes for which some persons who do not take responsibility wastes resources that others may need for the capability to function. It also denies persons the incentive to take responsibility for achieving the choices of which they are capable. As we shall consider, distinguishing lack of capability from squandered capabilities eludes precision that appears to be possible through measuring specific outcomes. Nevertheless, squandering capability is possible when persons persistently shirk responsibility for explicitly desired outcomes. Accountability by allowing persons to fall short of desired outcomes can foster capability for outcomes that persons choose. Accountability can engender capability. Judgment and accountability for desired outcomes for which persons are capable further augment their capability. If I know that I will not receive an educational degree unless I perform or will not achieve health benefits if I do not discipline my exercise or eating, that knowledge motivates me to take responsibility for my real opportunities for education and health. All of us have performed more capably when we are discretely judged or held accountable.

Examples illustrate these observations without offering specific numbers. Clearly, equally effective elementary and secondary (probably mandatory) education to ensure reading and numerical skills, a basic understanding of history and civic affairs, basic reasoning skills, minimal financial acumen, and appreciation for the arts is needed. These skills and functionings are all necessary to support a capability to choose and achieve another kind of or additional education and other functionings such as good health. Without basic education in reading, reasoning, and numerical skills, we are neither capable of nor know whether we want to be an educator or actuary, whether we want to accentuate or de-emphasize health for the sake of other outcomes. Nor are we capable of achieving the advanced education to become qualified for these professions or develop habits that enable a long and healthy life.

To continue with other illustrations: In today's US society, skilled childcare to enable preschool education and parents to work or volunteer in their communities is necessary for the capability to choose and achieve goals and well-being. Access to affordable housing in a secure neighborhood with good-quality schools is needed for families to seek any decent outcomes. Access to reasonably comprehensive high-quality healthcare and public health that provides healthy air and water and the ability to make reasonable decisions about addictive substances, nutrition, and exercise are also necessary. We are not capable of choosing excellent health or of activities for which good health is necessary without basic healthcare, public health information, and a healthy environment. None of these items is achievable without a basic structure that makes them affordable and accessible. They constitute basic capability; they cannot be left to free choice or individual responsibility. There is no freedom for choice without these basic capabilities, and no individual can be held responsible for choices and execution for which they are not capable.

Ensuring equal and basic capability of this kind does not require advanced education, investments in sophisticated education in financial skills or the arts, or the pinnacle of healthcare or good health. These matters can be left to individual choice and responsibility. However, the precise line between capability and taking responsibility for freely chosen outcomes cannot be specified with numerical precision. For example, some families and persons will be able to pay for preschool education and good healthcare and even some aspects of public health without government support, but many will not have the means to secure these goods without societal support. They are not being irresponsible or choosing an impoverished lifestyle. Society simply does not provide them the capability (or real opportunity) to choose a different life or take responsibility for it.

Conclusions

To account for these claims about the possibilities for changes in "natural" attributes as well as social circumstances, enabling new choices over time and overcoming disruptions (externally inflicted or self-inflicted), the basic structure supporting capability will have to respond to individual and group variations. Different alterable limits imposed by natural attributes and social circumstances will require various structural measures to expand choices and achievements. Decisions that foreclose new possibilities (e.g., stopping education and wanting to start again) and recoveries from disrupted lives (e.g., addictions that hinder good health or imprisonment that severely impedes future possibilities) will require structural and interpersonal interventions to enhance capability when it has been restricted. Individual choice and responsibility are not possible in these situations unless the basic structure fosters appropriate basic capability for persons.

To insist that self-development can produce the merits required for jobs, college admission, or some other position or recognition violates fair equality of opportunity. Fair opportunity requires help to enable actions beyond an individual's limited capability to development qualifications.

Science and social science are needed to inform us when the norm of equal or basic capability, or "real opportunity," is lacking and when and how fostering basic capability can create real opportunities. As research and technology develop and culture changes, what we can and are obligated to do to cultivate capability for persons evolves and becomes clearer. For example, we learn how to treat disabilities like autism and make the therapies accessible to all persons or how to adjust transportation systems and classrooms to compensate for physical and some intellectual impediments to opportunity.

FULLY FAIR EQUALITY OF OPPORTUNITY IS IMPOSSIBLE

A third barrier—beyond persons' choices about outcomes and possibility to take responsibility for their outcomes—arises because fully equal capability and fully fair opportunity are both impossible and even morally imprudent in some cases.

Let me explain. It is possible to imagine that Ernie Banks and I had equally valuable, although not identical, capability, and that I did not choose to or take responsibility for achieving the level he achieved in many areas of his life. Insofar as we can imagine that different levels of outcome are attributable to some taking greater responsibility for their functioning, we can affirm that persons with different levels of outcome have equal capability and opportunity, even as their outcomes are unequal. We can and should also acknowledge that our society has not done what it could structurally to foster equally valuable capability for many African Americans caught in our criminal justice system or for the high school–educated working-class families prevalent in much of the rural Midwest and South. If society could have done better to foster equal capability and did not, fair equality of opportunity is—or at least was—possible. Still, it is impossible to imagine what changes could nurture equally valuable capability for all persons fraught by devasting mental, physical, and psychological disabilities.

Examples of society and persons combining efforts over time to overcome these limitations warn us not to deny possibilities for equal capability too quickly. Think of Helen Keller and Stephen Hawking as high-profile examples. Society enhanced their capabilities, offering them capability for many choices and for executing those choices that they otherwise would not have had. Others, less widely known, have been given sufficient capability to achieve significant goals.

However, these anecdotal and inspiring examples do not deny the reality that current knowledge and techniques do not permit all disabled persons to possess capability even approaching that of Keller or

Hawking. Note that Keller and Hawking are not merely examples of heroic individuals overcoming unjust lack of opportunity. Society had to increase their capability for communication for them to achieve at their high level. They were persons enabled by the structure of society to excel when they would not have excelled in a less just structure—or at an earlier time, when therapeutic and other circumstances for support were not known. There are other examples of how enormous investments in persons with severe disabilities fostered significantly high levels of capability equally valuable with more typical members of society. Temple Grandin's high level of achievement with Asperger's syndrome, enabled by special educational provision for greater capability and revised cultural attitudes, is a high-profile example.

My point here is different. Societal structures cannot support equal or even basic capability in every such instance. Even a just basic structure and advances in therapeutic care and circumstances for greater capability cannot change that reality. The investments in capability exemplified in the paragraph above are justified and demanded by fair equality of opportunity, but unlimited investments on a broad level for everyone who can benefit from them—some only marginally—would, given current science and techniques, come at great cost to society. The costs can have severe consequences, not only for the common good but also for the prospect of equally valuable capability for those with different but similarly challenging difficulties. A form of cost-benefit analysis sensitive to justice for persons like Temple Grandin is necessary.[11]

Consider dementia, severe dyslexia, severe cerebral palsy, or Down syndrome as examples. The cost of bringing every person with significant maladies of these kinds to a capability level equal to, even though not identical with, typical persons in society would be enormous or impossible. So high, in fact, that it would greatly diminish societal capacity to foster the average capability of the entire population or the feasible capability of those with similar but less detrimental and more efficiently remedial afflictions. When these costs reach an exorbitant level, it may be morally preferable to fall short of what is possible in approximating equally valuable capability for all persons. I write this acknowledging that over time new discoveries may render these maladies more amenable to fully successful correction. We should always continue to encourage such developments.

This concession to consequentialism might be necessary even as we equally respect each citizen. It is never justified to withhold investment from groups—for example, minorities such as immigrants—in disfavor. It may, however, be more just to structure society to foster a level of capability that concedes a lower level of functioning, not the highest possible, to some severely disabled persons, thereby freeing resources to increase the average degree of capability for many, including other disabled persons. For example, the capability of persons with severe autism might be developed to permit choices for pursuing valuable outcomes without structural changes assuring the maximum possible opportunity. In these circumstances, they would have meaningful opportunities but not capabilities fully equal to those of average citizens or persons with less severe autism.

To understand this argument, we must recognize that capability is always a matter of degree. There is no absolute level of capability attainable for all members of society. Both individuals and citizens-on-average can have increased capabilities for outcomes from their choices and responsible efforts. The obligation to foster increases can never be absolute. We must also recognize that a commitment to equal capability—even equally valuable and not identical for everyone—interacts with the common good of society, including the average level of capability for all citizens. Fostering equal capability in all cases may also compete with respect for the capability of those with less severe capability deficits. Expenditures of time and funding to enable severely autistic persons to function at their maximum possible level could reduce resources devoted to education and therapy that fosters the capability of many other citizens, for example, those with mild dyslexia. Our failure to maximize capability for any individual or group is always lamentable, but so is devoting maximum resources to some group to achieve limited results when those resources are diverted from equally deserving individuals and groups for whom the efforts could be more effective.

Note well: This kind of analysis does not contend that there is no obligation to severely disabled persons or that society should withdraw support from anyone due to their irresponsible behavior. I have not withdrawn my earlier claim that we have responsibilities to persons who have behaved irresponsibly. These disabled persons have not necessarily been irresponsible. In addition, the analysis employed here does not weigh the cost of help to a few disabled persons against overall benefits, especially not economic benefits, to society. Yet equal opportunity should not be an absolute standard without regard to any prudential considerations.

This understanding of capability as opportunity differs from equal opportunity for the most qualified by outlawing extraneous prejudices based on a disfavored group. Prejudices against disfavored groups with equal qualifications can never by justified. Failing to invest in increased capabilities for some groups never permits discrimination violating the principle of positions open to the most—or at least to reasonably well-qualified—applicants. On the other hand, enhancing capability may be possible but not pursued because of enormous costs to many other persons in society. These costs are not principally monetary or measured by GDP. They can be in the form of reduced opportunities of others for civic involvement, leisure time, or community action. In some cases, achieving the highest possible capability for some persons can reduce the opportunities of many others to pursue outcomes of their choosing.

It is possible for investments in capability for groups to enhance or diminish the prospects for average capability or for other groups who would benefit from effective investments to nurture their capability. Dollars and policies directed to improving the criminal justice system may augment the security and capability of racial minorities and the working poor more than dollars and regulations invested in disabilities more difficult to overcome and affecting smaller numbers of citizens. Difficult judgments in these areas are messy, but they may be just if they are based on the best available science and social science and never reject respect for the dignity of every person and group. We need good science and social science to understand the effectiveness and efficiency of these comparative investments.

For example, we can learn from comparing the long-term value of dialysis and kidney transplants for expanding capability to what sound therapy can achieve for children with different degrees of autism. We can also invest in renal disease and autism research with the prospect of increasing capability for persons in the future. These are ways in which science and social science are vitally important to maximizing fair equality of opportunity. But note also that normative judgments about the equal dignity of all persons and special consideration for those who have been previously deprived of equal capability inform the use of science here. Equal opportunity is not relegated to the findings of science only.

Granting that capability is always a matter of degree, there is of course another dimension that justifies doing less than is possible for some individuals and groups. The current discussion of privilege highlights this phenomenon. We can—and do to some extent—invest in expanding capability to choose and execute outcomes for those who are already privileged by greater than equal capability. Here again, prudent cost-benefit considerations obtain. We can squander public resources by subsidizing marginally beneficial education for the well-off or by protecting housing and security—for example, with mortgage interest tax deductions for opulent houses of those who already have adequate housing and secure neighborhoods rather than for modest housing and security for those less well-off.

We must, however, take care not to confuse achievement with privilege. The achievements of many, including those with reasonably high-level outcomes, is not always due to excessive privilege. In addition, we should not deny special treatment for those whose demonstrated or likely outcomes enhance the capabilities or outcomes for many others and increase the capability of all persons. Consider again in this context Rawls's "difference principle" in which the unequal benefits to some lead to greater fostering of capability for many others, especially the least well-off. As noted previously, the unequal benefits to those whose work benefits others may be in forms other than income, for example, recognition that gives satisfaction. If, for example, providing greater benefits (not necessarily income) and capability to secondary school educators offers the least well-off more opportunities, we may well be justified in promoting greater than equally valuable capabilities for secondary school educators.

Here one might also think of public expenditures that increase the capability of a scientist who benefits autistic children or diabetics. Or, with some qualifications, an Elon Musk who advances renewable energy, keeping in mind that Musk may be an example of a person who demands some privileges that do not enhance his capability to benefit others. We are all more or less privileged by the capabilities society and other individuals grant us. Recognizing that capability comes in degrees rather than a set amount requires that we be alert to the prospect that special privilege and opportunities supported by public expenditures may or may not be justified by the positive consequences for many other persons.

To accurately understand trade-offs among different investments in capability, we must keep in mind the distinction between investments for capability and investments for economic output. Recall again Amartya Sen's distinction between human capability and human capital. Investments and return on investments in capability are not measured by monetary investments and monetary output alone. These cost-benefit calculations are not measured in monetary terms alone. The pertinent issue pertaining to an Elon Musk is whether his contributions to clean energy for transportation benefit the climate and others less well-off, especially the least well-off, and not whether it increases GDP. Consider also my example of investing in the capability of secondary school teachers whose work will not necessarily increase GDP.

The measure of outcomes requires increasing contributions to public health knowledge and changing cultural perspectives on deservedness, for example, of addicts. Society may reduce GDP by investing to change treatment of and cultural attitudes toward aspects of addiction but increase the capability and opportunities for many addicts. Money is a factor in these investments, but so are time, institutional practices, regulations, and policies. We are not measuring results by GDP or any collective economic outcome. We are asking how these various investments nurture capability that affects the overall average capability and the distribution of levels of capability among identifiable groups.

As I write, we are discovering the relative cost of the COVID-19 virus and the relative benefits of remedial actions to different racial, class, occupational, and geographical groups. The measurements are in terms of life expectancy, group unemployment, health status, educational advancement, and housing cost (not merely income per capita or total GDP). There is indeed a cost-benefit trade-off, but these outcomes are compared and capability is measured in terms of a range of opportunities and the distribution of capabilities among different groups. These considerations transcend and are more complex than measurements in terms of collective income or wealth outcomes only. For example, investing in housing and public transportation that exposes working class families to fewer contagious diseases and supports safer communities may be justified despite collective economic cost.

In 2022, Mayor Lightfoot of Chicago issued a press release publicizing action by the City Council for a transportation program she claimed focused on bringing safe, walkable, and vibrant communities to poorer areas on Chicago's Southside. She explicitly referred to more equal access to safe transportation among wealthy and poorer communities. Whether or not that action produced a redistribution to expand opportunities for vulnerable communities, the rhetoric about equalizing transportation between wealthy communities on the Northside and poorer communities affirms a laudable aspiration to invest in transportation in ways that expand opportunities for the poorer communities.[12]

The upshot remains that neither absolutely equal capability nor maximum capability is obtainable. Maximizing the capability of the most advantaged is not always or even usually increasing fair and equal opportunity. Nor can a society rest easy that it has achieved the ideal of equal basic capability. Adjustments—for example, in therapy for addicts—are always possible and necessary. There is, however, a normative principle: equal respect for the capability and opportunity of each person in society. A trade-off to neglect the capability of persons in highly disadvantageous social circumstances or with a nearly intractable malady like severe autism or addiction in order to maximize average capability or the capability of some other favored group is unjust. However, refraining from maximum efforts to increase the capability of some disadvantaged groups to the highest level possible if it diminishes the average capability of many others may be justified. This approach should enhance equal respect for the capability and opportunity of all persons.

Curtailing subsidies and regulations that grant increased capabilities of the already highly privileged can, if their opportunities redound to the benefit of many, detract from overall fair equality of opportunity. Perhaps research subsidies for electric vehicle entrepreneurs will benefit public health and overall average as well as approximately equal capability, not because it augments GDP but because it allows for better health outcomes for most citizens. Good data and fair cost-benefits analysis are vital.

Adopting capability as the measure of fair opportunity must be realistic in both what it proposes and what can be achieved. The combination of (1) limits on the malleability of individual nature and circumstances, (2) respect for freedom to choose desire outcomes, and (3) the expectation that individuals exercise responsibility to achieve what they choose renders completely equal and maximum fair opportunity impossible. A form of cost-benefit analysis that considers the extent of some likely enhancements of capability and how they affect the capabilities of others is necessary. We cannot get beyond this impasse and still respect individual self-identity, freedom, responsibility, and moral prudence.

I am clearly not advocating for the often-cited dictum "Let justice be done though the heavens fall." Nevertheless, an approximation of fair equality of opportunity that affirms the imperative of universal self-respect is consistent with a realistic understanding of how the structure of society affects fair equality of opportunity.

I realize that these considerations rule out principles that dictate a specific structure for fair equality of opportunity. There are no absolute just conclusions. We cannot conclude that precise policies exist for achieving a structure or that absolute equality of opportunity is even possible. That admitted, we are not left without principles of justice that commit us to policies that respect fair opportunity for each person, especially for the most vulnerable.

A special kind of cost-benefit enters our deliberations to affirm and discover the closest approximation of respect for equal capability for each person to choose and take responsibility for the outcomes they favor. This method enables us to use the best data regarding promising research and methods for approximating fair equality of opportunity. Data can show, for example, that education that adjusts for specific learning disabilities expands persons' capabilities for multiple outcomes. That data, albeit uncertain, can show that the cost of these adjustments should be considered so as not to preclude effective expansion of capabilities for others. Data can also show the promise of research to expand persons' capabilities in the future. We are not left with definitive answers to issues of structural policy, but we are provided normative guidance for what fair equality of opportunity requires and for the kind of social scientific data we need to maximize approximation of that principle. The common economic good does not override respect for each individual, especially the most vulnerable.[13] We are left with clear guidance for research and reasoned discourse regarding the specific issues we must consider to approximate the normative principle of equal capability and opportunity for all.[14]

Limits on the Freedom to Choose Outcomes

We are nearly ready to consider more-specific issues about how a society and people can approximate fair equality of opportunity. But as adumbrated earlier, these proposals must be made within the restraints that citizens and residents have on their choices about what outcomes fair opportunity permits them to pursue. These limits go well beyond curtailing explicit and implicit tendencies to inject extraneous factors into judgments about who is qualified for a position or opportunity.[15] Citizens who choose to pursue their favored outcomes without regard to how their pursuit affects the basic or equal capabilities of others violate the robust conception of fair equality of opportunity proposed here.

This fault includes those who seek to maximize their disposable income without considering how government revenue is needed for investments in childcare, healthcare, public health, housing, and education to foster basic capability for all. They undermine fair equality of opportunity. All citizens should support these public investments. They are not morally free—and should not be legally free—to oppose them for the sake of increased income and wealth for themselves. Similarly, those who oppose or disregard environmental regulations for the sake of short-term economic growth jeopardize the basic health and well-being of the most disadvantaged citizens (current and future). These citizens lose capability to choose good health and the possibility of a long life. Other examples include those who favor zoning regulations that sustain neighborhood housing values and schools segregated by race and class and those who insist on smoking or not wearing masks in a closed public setting or resist vaccinations that protect others during a pandemic.

In sum, all citizens are obligated to promote both individual behavior and structures that expand equal capability for fair opportunity, even if those obligations limit choices about outcomes they may desire and seek to realize for themselves. Approximating fair equality of opportunity is not consonant with libertarianism in which individuals advance their own outcomes without considering fostering opportunities for others.[16]

Citizens and residents must willingly comply with adjustments to the basic structure that limit choice about what outcomes they may pursue, because fostering equal capability requires these limits on individual and even associational freedom. The latter suggests that civic and religious groups are not justly free to ignore the obligations of fair equality of opportunity. They should not pursue group ends in conflict with equal opportunity for all. For example, in some instances during a pandemic, churches may not gather for weddings and funerals without jeopardizing the opportunity of many for health and life.

These freedoms should be restrained voluntarily in two specific ways. First, citizens must exceed mere compliance with just law to work for a more just system. They must acknowledge and support additional structural accommodations needed to foster capability. For example, all citizens should support community efforts to promote better security for minorities and for those who are economically and culturally disadvantaged by the criminal justice system. Unfortunately and unjustly, some persons can be denied security due to policing and judicial processes and sentencing, unhealthy and unnecessarily lengthy incarcerations, or long paroles without full citizen rights. Citizens and associations must work to support healthcare and public health policies that bolster citizens' and residents' capability for good health. We are not free to remain complacent about structural injustices that maintain these and other unjustified constraints on opportunity.

Second, fair equality of opportunity requires interpersonal actions by family members, associates in employment, fellow citizens, and friends that affirm the social bases for self-respect and help renew broken capability. This interpersonal behavior includes offering forgiveness when it is fitting and needed to restore capability. These limits on freedom—or, better, efforts to use freedom for positive fostering of capability for others—differ from compliance with and support for coercive structural policies. These behaviors are morally induced and not legally enforced or even enforceable. The acts I have in mind—for example, effective judgment of and forgiveness for a wayward family member or a friend who has disrupted relationships by addictions or effective affirmation of a self-doubting subordinate or associate in the workplace—cannot be enforced by structural arrangements. They require individual initiatives, although structures can cultivate cultures to encourage these individual actions. These can be individual moral obligations and simultaneously necessary for the fair opportunity of others to choose and achieve new outcomes. In this regard, I differ from those, like John Rawls, who limit what justice requires to the basic structure of society independent of individual and associational behavior.[17]

We are now ready to consider who lacks fair equality of opportunity, why, and more specific structures and individual actions needed to achieve a maximum approximation of equal capability for all.

NOTES

1. That does not negate the likelihood that the comprehensive religious vision initiated these dispositions toward culpable persons in need of grace and continues to have a role in sustaining them.

2. See Michael J. Sandel, *The Tyranny of Merit*, p. 227.

3. Norman Daniels—see *Just Health: Meeting Health Needs Fairly* (New York: Cambridge University Press, 2008)—includes health in fair opportunity; Ronald Dworkin proposes equal resources in "What Is Equality? Part 2: Equality of Resources," *Philosophy & Public Affairs 10/4 (1981)*: 283–345; and Ruth Faden and Madison Powers, *Structural Injustice: Power, Advantage, and Human Rights* (New York: Oxford University Press, 2019), propose a threshold level of six "core elements" for well-being. I will not discuss the philosophical arguments underlying these different proposals, but my own understandings are informed by these and other sources, even though I do not agree with them in total or incorporate them fully into my argument.

4. Sen and Nussbaum believe that at least some capacities can be improved to bolster capabilities to qualify for positions that enable persons to achieve their desired outcomes. Limited capacities are given, not cultivated. Think of persons limited by autism or near blindness. As observed previously, not all capacities are unchangeable, although some may be subject to limited enhancement by fostering capabilities.

5. As I reread this sentence, I am reminded of a remark by Meghan Markle to Oprah Winfrey about how Ms. Markle was affected by casual comments from members of the Royal Family, or the "Firm," expressing concern about how dark Ms. Markle's offspring would be. The apparent effect on Ms. Markle's sense of self-respect and capability for functioning were palpable for all who heard the interview, even though the remarks were interpersonal and not dictated by a "basic structure."

6. These observations rely on *The Color of Law: A Forgotten History of How Our Government Segregated America* by Richard Rothstein (New York: W. W. Norton & Company, 2017). The book has implications for ideological disputes about legally supported and systematic racism, but insofar as I recall, Rothstein does not mention CRT or any other theory. He relies on specific empirical evidence applied to different laws, structures, and times in American history, and a reader who does not concur with every specific argument should

nonetheless be persuaded by much of Rothstein's evidence for widespread de jure segregation.

7. Use of the concept talents must be further qualified, because what constitutes an innate talent depends on demands in changing circumstances rather than talents in some absolute unchanging sense. For example, a talent for brain surgery would not have been of much value in the eighteenth century, and a talent to hit a baseball would not have been of value in the early nineteenth century. In both instances, what constitutes talent is determined by changing circumstances, not by a permanent eternally valuable natural talent of the surgeon or athlete.

We should also note again here that outcomes might not be in terms of income. The surgeon or baseball player may receive other outcomes of unequal value—for example, public recognition or respect to induce them to develop their talents to benefit others. Rawls's distributive principle, in my judgment, focuses too narrowly on income.

8. See *From Neurons to Neighborhoods: The Science of Early Childhood Development* from the National Research Council Institute of Medicine (Washington, DC: National Academy Press, 2000), for a comprehensive and well-vetted study of the interplay between nature and nurture as they apply to development among children. Also note that this interplay changes over time, enabling even greater intervention to promote capability relative to nature.

9. We should also note that the outcomes for Banks and Gates are different even though they may be equally valuable. Income may be unequal for accomplished professional athletes and high-profile scholars, while job satisfaction and other benefits are equal or even greater for the scholar. We are reminded, once again, that income is not the sole measure of desired outcomes.

10. Both philosophers and theologians hold nuanced judgments regarding effort, merit, and responsibility. John Rawls and Michael Sandel grant that effort is enabled by forces beyond an individual agent. I concur. Many theologians insist that effort is a product of grace or nurturing by others—a gifted capability and not solely attributable to individual merit. I agree with this view also. That does not mean we have nothing to do with our efforts to execute a task or project. Even the most predestinarian Christian theologians—John Calvin included—rejected the claim that dependence on divine grace precludes willing and responsibility. Grace *enables* us to will and take responsibility, but each agent also wills and takes responsibility for what they will.

11. I do not intend to imply that the attention offered to Dr. Grandin was a mis-expenditure of time or funds. If for no other reason, her success is an example of what may be possible. Cost-benefit analysis applied to disabilities is complex and should never undermine respect for the dignity of a disabled person or group. It is open to error, and facile dismissal of individual cases or even of group support is always mistaken.

12. See "City Council Passes the Connected Communities Ordinance to Grow Economy, Make Streets Safer, and Promote Affordability," July 20, 2022, www.chicago.gov/city/en/depts/mayor/press_room/press_releases/2022/july/PassesConnectedCommunitiesOrdinance.html.

13. I am reminded in this context of legislators who insisted that the US Congress cut back on the deficit by eliminating assistance for families and children in need rather than by increasing taxes paid by the most well-off citizens.

14. Readers with a modest knowledge of the discipline of ethics will recognize the implied claim that duty to respect individual persons can be combined with a form of cost-benefit analysis that seeks to maximize a version of the good for all. Fortunately, we do not need to follow the scholarly tension between deontological and utilitarian ethics to understand why a specific version of cost-benefit calculations can enhance respect for the dignity of every person.

15. Readers my age will remember when Lester Maddox, former governor of Georgia in the early seventies, refused to serve Blacks in his Atlanta restaurant simply because of the color of their skin. The constraints on freedoms we are considering in this context include but go far beyond the restraints on racial prejudice Governor Maddox claimed interfered with his freedom. Younger readers may think of the Colorado website designer who the Supreme Court granted the freedom to reject any request from a same-sex couple for website services of any kind.

16. I reiterate that none of these restraints on individual freedom required by justice obviates the liberty of every person, family, or associate, to pursue their own outcomes or vision of well-being consistent with what fair equality of opportunity demands of them. They may even pursue different moral objectives beyond the constrains of justice—for example, special generosity to neighbors and distant persons.

17. I emphasize that freedoms to pursue different actions based on moral considerations still exist within these individual constraints required by justice. Fair equality of opportunity may require that I forgive a neighbor and encourage another to sustain self-respect consonant with engendering basic capability for opportunity but still allow me freedom to pursue different moral paths regarding which civic organization should command my time or money. Not all moral matters are subject to the institutional restraints of justice.

Chapter 3

Approximating Fair Equality of Opportunity in the United States

First, we must identify who is denied fair opportunity and what interactions and structures perpetuate unjust inequality of opportunity. Changes in interactions and structures are required to establish just opportunity because the status quo is not fair. Positive initiatives, not merely a prohibition of unfair discrimination, are required. While my proposal for fair equality of opportunity does not permit extrapolating from all unequal outcomes to determine injustice, it permits considering some unequal outcomes unjust. First, persons or groups denied basic capability for choices about what additional outcomes they can pursue may justly claim for society to foster their minimal capabilities. All of us should join in this demand for minimum capability for opportunity. Without these minimal outcomes, there can be no real opportunity based on qualifications. This claim for structural justice stands in stark contrast to the claim that persons without minimum support for food, health, housing, and education have an opportunity to pursue their own well-being, and if they do not, they are responsible for their own outcomes. Lyndon Johnson was right when he declared at Howard University following the passage of the 1964 civil rights legislation that it is inadequate to declare to those disadvantaged by many encumbrances, "You are [now] free to compete with all the others." Equal opportunity takes more than barring Lester Maddox from turning away African Americans from his restaurant.

The essential means for basic capability include minimal income, a sound high school education, reasonably good public health support, and assured adequate healthcare. Public health includes attention to good nutrition. It also includes provision for physical, mental, and emotional development, especially for children from conception forward with special, but not exclusive, concern for early years.[1] Support for stable families is part of this aspect of public health. Public health also promotes an environment free from unnecessary health (including mental health) hazards to which the most vulnerable members of society (racial minorities, persons concentrated in lower social economic status neighborhoods, and groups in remote geographical areas) are often unjustly subjected. Protection from the most detrimental and disruptive effects of climate change are part of this public health for equal basic opportunity. All persons should have access to at least modestly compensated employment with adequate provision for parental and sick leave. This access includes the option to gain skills for employment and access to inexpensive, high-quality childcare, freeing parents for employment.

Minimal capability for opportunity also requires access to safe and secure housing in proximity to good public schools and places of employment. Equal capability includes security from violence directed at neighborhoods and identifiable groups. Having long commutes to work with poor public transportation denies minimal capability. In addition, minimal capability provides for efforts to remedy disabilities as that becomes feasible and to adjust circumstances to minimize these disadvantages. Finally, it ensures a criminal justice system that provides security and does not harass and unjustly discriminate against those without adequate standing in a community. In many cases, racial and class groups and persons living in remote geographical areas suffer disproportionately from the absence of many of these minimum capabilities.

I reiterate for emphasis: It is not a response to policies to assure these minimal capabilities to retort that persons and groups who do not have them are responsible for their own plight. They may be in some fashion responsible, but they do not have an equal opportunity to overcome these deficits if they lack minimum provisions. Lavish outcomes are not helpful for persons who have been irresponsible, but recall my contention that justice requires opportunity even for those who have shirked previous opportunities. Making grace and forgiveness available for all demand it. Denying children's nutritional programs such as WIC and

SNAP contingent on parental employment, Medicaid contingent on employment, basic rights of citizenship after incarceration, and other programs to foster basic capability are never justified.

When society fails to foster these minimal outcomes, freedom from unjust discrimination that bars choices by unfair measurements of qualifications is not the principal obstacle to opportunity. Rather, the basic capability to choose among and execute outcomes is denied by the basic structure and/or the failure of other persons to contribute needs to foster minimum basic capability. Some persons experiencing these circumstances may have acted irresponsibly (e.g., rejected reasonable employment or housing support) or have been disadvantaged by random fate that cannot be remedied (e.g., a disease or accident that has irreversibly affected their outcomes). Even in these cases, withholding what is minimally necessary to foster basic capability denies real opportunity.

It is not possible that entire groups are disproportionately irresponsible or suffer negative random fates, and even where irresponsibility explains the lack of minimal support to foster capability, judgment that precludes adequate opportunity runs counter to justice. In fact, where many persons from any group fail to attain these minimal outcomes, it is due to societal failure to foster their basic capability. In some isolated cases, family members, individual citizens, or civic organizations may have failed to provide what only they can offer, but society should still do what it can to compensate for these individual failures, for example, a delinquent parent or spouse or an abusive workplace associate. Even if subcultural factors are at work among some groups, they are usually the consequence of unjust structures or individual discrimination that social structures have not adequately remedied. Structural factors or failures of positive interpersonal support have limited the means to basic capability and thus to real opportunity.

Even when individuals or groups have been irresponsible or suffered bad luck, society should, if feasible, provide minimal outcomes that enable basic capability for their renewal. That may require provision for minimal income, access to employment, nutrition, healthcare (including mental health and addiction therapy), support for families, a continued basic education, training for employment, decent housing and supports for a secure neighborhood, and protection from violence. In some cases, it will require acts of personal or institutional forgiveness, although forgiveness is unnecessary and inappropriate if persons or groups are victims of previous injustice and without fault. In these cases, they need appropriate reparation, which may not be—most often is not—merely in the form of income. Income is often not the best means for establishing minimal basic capability.

Reparation by income transfer may focus on a singular outcome with little consideration for how that outcome enhances basic capability for fair opportunity. Retraining for employment, healthcare, or provision for housing and education may be more effective than mere dollars. These provisions should not be conditioned on behavior—except avoiding future violations of the law. They should be effective means for basic capability to renew real opportunities. For example, the evidence increasingly demonstrates that unconditional and refundable child tax credits encourage parental childcare and employment. To be effective, initiatives of renewal and forgiveness require agents to readily respond and seize opportunities. But even unresponsive agents need to be sustained until they are ready to reciprocate. Providing nutrition and health is unconditionally essential. Even recalcitrant homeless persons who reject housing and accompanying support need minimal nutrition, healthcare, and community support to be ready to respond responsibly to fostering new capabilities. These are not instances in which irresponsibility fully explains subpar outcomes. These bad outcomes are rarely freely chosen.

MINIMAL INCOME

We know that children who spend sustained periods in households with income below the poverty threshold are far less likely to receive adequate education, nutrition, and health. Persons might choose to sacrifice income for other outcomes. They rarely choose income below what is needed to make choices about their education, their nutrition, their family structure, their qualifications for employment, their healthcare, and so on. That income level is visited upon them by circumstances they cannot change (even if it may be partially their own irresponsibility, which is never the case for children and rarely the case for adults).

Let me reiterate for clarity: Even if a person or family lacking minimal income is not hindered by explicit prejudicial discrimination, they lack the minimum capability for opportunity. The person or family lacks opportunity simply by lacking minimal income to enable them to choose and achieve greater income and other desirable outcomes. These persons lack basic capability to envision and execute choices. Moreover, even a blameworthy person who lacks this minimal income has no real opportunity to change the course of their life—and the outcomes for their family. A just society owes that person sufficient income to establish or reestablish minimum capability.

The 2022 Census Bureau report on poverty shows that 11.6 percent of US residents lived in families below the official poverty line in 2021 based on a threshold established in the early 1960s. The threshold was set as an income below three times a minimal food budget. It was intended to measure a minimal level of income for a modestly decent existence, which I have claimed is one criterion for basic capability for real opportunity. This official threshold varies according to the number of family members and whether adults or children compose the family. In 2021, it was $13,788 for a single household head and approximately $27,740 for a four-person household, depending on the persons composing the family. Most concerning, in 2021, 15 percent of children under the age of eighteen in the United States lived in households below the official poverty threshold.

These official poverty measurements came under increasing criticism for failure to count noncash benefits such as SNAP (food stamps) and tax credits, but also increasing necessary expenses, such as out-of-pocket healthcare and expenses connected with working. The official thresholds also failed to adjust adequately for changing essential expenses incurred by families. In 2010, the Census Bureau made adjustments, publishing the first Supplemental Poverty Measure (SPM) in 2011 and then annually. The SPM accounts for noncash benefits; changing expenses for food, clothing, shelter, and utilities;[2] and unavoidable expenses related to working (childcare costs are not included) and healthcare. In the past, the SPM poverty rate has been marginally higher than the official poverty rate or measure (OFM). (The in-kind benefits and tax credits reduce poverty, but the higher threshold and inclusion of necessary work and healthcare expenses increase the poverty rate.)

There is some good news among this empirical data. For 2021, the SPM rate, at 7.8 percent, was down substantially from 2020 and is now significantly below the OFM. The decrease in the SPM child poverty rate is even more remarkable. From 2020 to 2021, it declined from

9.7 percent (down from 12.6 percent in 1219) to 5.2 percent, the lowest on record for the SPM, and now well below the OFM rate (15 percent).[3] The SPM includes items that primarily benefit children. (The SPM poverty rate was below the official poverty rate for the first time in 2020, although the SPM rate for children has been slightly lower than the official rate in the past.)

The precipitous declines in these SPM measures are due in large part to the SPM including in-kind benefits and refundable taxes. These benefits were especially large in 2020–21 due to COVID-related assistance, but they are also influenced by recent efforts to reduce child-income poverty. Note, for example, the bipartisan recommendations for reducing child poverty in *A Roadmap to Reducing Child Poverty* (see note 1). There is no assurance that these relatively low rates will persist as the stimulus and child tax credits related to COVID-19 diminish, but they are not confined to COVID-stimulated efforts either.

By the standards of the nearly forty members of the Organisation for Economic Co-operation and Development, the poverty and child-poverty rates in the United States still rank high. Although the OECD threshold is set differently and relative to the median income of households rather than an absolute income amount, based on 2021 data the United States ranked worse than most countries in overall poverty and a little worse than Mexico, equal with Romania, and better than only Turkey, Chile, Israel, Costa Rica, and South Africa in child poverty.[4]

Data also shows that the percentage of those below minimal income is not equally distributed among demographic groups. African Americans, Hispanics, immigrants, persons from outside of metropolitan areas, single-parent households (especially but not only those with female heads), those without a high school degree, and disabled adults all have higher poverty rates. Children under eighteen have traditionally been in poor households at a higher rate than persons over eighteen and still are according to the OFM, although not the SPM.[5] I reiterate that these persons do not choose alternative outcomes over minimal income or minimum in-kind help. They do not have the capability to choose leisure, service, or family time over minimum income. That is because minimal income and in-kind support are necessary for the opportunity to choose and achieve higher income or non-income outcomes.

Let's remember, we are not merely considering unequal income but also an income and in-kind support level below a threshold that enables choice for more income or other desirable outcomes. Although some individuals from each group may have failed to take responsibility for achieving the income they are capable of receiving, demographic groups are not disproportionately irresponsible. We should look to structural injustices, rather than focusing on explicitly invidious discrimination against groups, as principal causes of this disproportionality. Personal discrimination detrimental to members of minority groups continues, but disproportional fostering of capability by structures, as we have seen, is almost certainly more significant.

Furthermore, we should seek means for ensuring that even irresponsible persons—and all families—receive this minimal income equivalent. It enables a capability to choose and execute better outcomes. Increases in income without employment is not a disincentive for better outcomes when the provision for minimal existence is so inadequate that it makes renewed opportunity impossible. Persons without minimum nutrition, housing, provision for their health, and security have insufficient opportunity to choose and increase their income as well as other outcomes through employment.

Remedies

A variety of structural changes might reduce this high percentage of the US population lacking minimal income for basic capability. There is of course an option of distributing cash or more in-kind funds to those below a poverty threshold. Effective policies could include universal basic income grants, nutrition funding (especially SNAP and WIC for children), refundable child tax credits, childcare subsidies, healthcare support, housing and rent subsidies, unemployment compensation, workers' compensation, and disability grants. Increases of in-kind assistance, as measured by the SPM, especially in response to COVID, help explain its significant decrease in the poverty rate. An additional raise in legal minimum wage and the Earned Income Tax Credit (EITC) for poorly compensated workers can help bring some families, if they are employed, above the poverty income threshold.

Some contend that a minimum wage can cause unemployment, which it no doubt does if it is high enough, but that claim has to be demonstrated by empirical evidence, not on ideological grounds. Multiple empirical studies demonstrate that modest changes in the minimum wage have minimal effects on unemployment. The EITC has the disadvantage of public subsidies for selected employers, who may fail to accept adequate responsibility for improving the productivity of and compensation for their employees. For example, if the EITC brings McDonald's employees above the poverty line, taxpayers, rather than McDonald's, pay the cost. If employees are brought to a minimum acceptable income by EITC, the employer makes no contribution and is instead subsidized by taxpayers. This description applies especially to employers with high percentages of low-wage workers. Public funds rather than the employers and the consumers of their products are forced to pay for higher income levels for these poorly paid employees. EITC may still be the most politically prudent and economically efficient means for increasing income for some poorly compensated workers, but it should not be used without considering its undesirable consequences. It is not a singular means for reducing income poverty.

Guaranteeing jobs through public employment at the local, state, or federal level has demonstrated success in assuring both employment and advancement of the public good that would otherwise fail to be realized. New investments in infrastructure of roads and other transportation needs have already proven to raise employment and income levels for primarily high school graduates and working-class citizens. Some of these structural supports could have other benefits for real opportunity by enhancing personal and public health, housing, and security or assuring accessible employment. Unconditional subsidies might discourage employment, but that must be tested empirically rather than simply asserted by ideologically inspired economic theory. Even if they do discourage employment in some cases, they may foster basic capabilities for functioning. Increasing the number of persons who attain a high school education, also required for basic capability for outcomes beyond a minimal income, would help persons achieve a minimal income. Public policies can also bolster the prospects for families, including single-parent families, to receive greater compensation through employment. For example, childcare subsidies and a child tax credit not only provide greater household income but also can improve family harmony and the capability of single-parents, especially mothers, to work for income.

This list of ways to provide cash or in-kind resources does not resolve all the issues about what means are most prudent and fair to provide a near-universal minimum income. It does indicate that lack of minimum income is largely a structural injustice.[6] It cannot be resolved simply by imploring persons to get jobs or by negative incentives to induce persons and families who lack capability to earn the income they desire or by stimulating the economy to increase GDP.

Although these policies may require increased and more-progressive taxes, any unfairness these taxes suggest should be balanced by the consequences of denying fair equality of opportunity to those below a minimal income. Even if increased progressive taxes reduce overall economic growth, we have seen that increases in GDP are less morally significant than fair equality of opportunity. The impediments to opportunity are more profound than either economic growth, which is necessary but insufficient for opportunity, or eradicating disincentives for responsible economic behavior, which is not a significant factor at minimal levels of income. This minimal income support leaves persons with more capability to gain employment and little disincentive to seek greater remuneration through employment.

In sum, multiple structural changes could enhance the capability of families and individuals to receive the minimum income required for the basic capability to make choices for other outcomes, including higher income, family participation, education, civic participation, and leisure. Fair equality of opportunity demands these significant structural reforms to assure more—almost all—of the population receives a minimum income. I acknowledge that there may always be a small percentage of irredeemably irresponsible persons for whom there is no feasible prudent way to ensure this income or render it an efficient means for basic capability. There will always be a few individuals who will not use the income capability to advance their functioning. Even so, there is no reason to abandon efforts to assure a minimum income for every individual or family.

Additional structural changes may mitigate homelessness and mental health disabilities to bring additional persons to a minimum income level. It is not possible to identify what persons or families are irredeemably irresponsible or beyond effective efforts to bolster minimum capability. Hence, a variety of policies—not all of them focused on income—are needed to increase fair opportunity for all.

MINIMAL EDUCATION

Lack of minimal income is, of course, only one basic capability denying choice and opportunity. According to Statista, nearly 9 percent
of the US population had not completed a high school degree in
2021.[7] Various data show that the rate of high school graduation for
Blacks and Hispanics in the United States is a few percentage points
lower than the average and that Native American rates are still lower.

A high school education can help achieve minimal income[8] and
enable choices about additional income in balance with other outcomes.
The income consequences are not, however, the only reason for minimal education to expand capability. Apart from its impact on income
levels, a high school education or its equivalent is necessary to make
choices about more formal education, health, political and civic participation, types of employment, family life, and more. Individuals without
a high school education often lack basic capability for real opportunity,
whether or not they have sufficient income for opportunity.

Studies demonstrate a clear link between lack of a high school
degree and morbidity and early mortality, as well as an unstable family
life. Angus Deaton and Anne Case cite extensive data demonstrating
these links and show that they apply to Caucasians as well as to African
Americans.[9] In fact, lack of education seems to have had an increasingly
deleterious effect on Caucasian health and families, although African
Americans still suffer disproportionately from negative outcomes in
these areas. It is possible, of course, that income alone explains these
differences in health and family stability. It could be that those in this
cohort (i.e., those without a high school degree) choose unhealthy life-
styles and disruptive family life or are disproportionately irresponsible
in executing their choices. Neither explanation, however, adequately
explains the differences or the recent trends cited by Case and Deaton
and others.[10]

Remedies

Data from many economists, perhaps most notably Nobel Prize–winner
James Heckman, examining the effects of early childhood education
demonstrate that high-quality early childhood education has a positive
effect on increasing continuation in school to achieve a high school

degree or its equivalent. Head Start is of course the most well-known, but it's not the only program for early childhood education. It is not universal.[11] Household stability and caring support for children are also major factors fostering completion of a high school education. Children from a stable family, ideally two-parent (same or different genders) households, are also more likely to receive a high school degree. Some observers attribute household stability solely to responsible individual behavior, but this simple explanation fails to note the toll that a lack of childcare and inadequate maternity and paternity leave can take on families. For low-income families, public regulations (e.g., a minimum wage) and expenditures to support parenting (e.g., refundable child tax credits for children and the Earned Income Tax Credit) enhance the prospects of a stable family life for children.

A particular family structure (e.g., two-parent households and stable family environments) are not necessary for opportunities for other outcomes. Nevertheless, family structure and family life play a significant role for children living in households with a minimally acceptable income and in their achieving a minimal education. Hence, public policy and interactive support from family and friends, libertarian objections to support for specific family types notwithstanding, have a fundamental role in contributing to this aspect of fair equality of opportunity.

Greg Duncan and Richard Murnane wrote a volume and edited another with many prominent authors focused on education and opportunity. Their exploration extends into post-secondary education, but in addition to the factors mentioned previously, the authors call for changes in elementary and secondary education. They consider smaller schools and classrooms, increased accountability for teachers and schools, responses to student psychological and behavioral problems, addressing disabilities, neighborhood influences, ensuring available family funds, and school safety. They also consider school funding. Funding support and equality are significant but insufficient. Funding should not be the exclusive focus. Here is also an occasion for more help for financial and other supports for elementary school teachers that are not impoverished. Such provisions that benefit them are likely to benefit those less well off without real opportunities.

Even though preschool education and stable family and parental support are important, these structural changes in schools (including intervention to help individual students and problem schools) should also be considered. So should increasing families' monetary resources. For example, better wages for families and nutritional supports are needed to improve student retention and graduation rates. These factors can improve the quality of elementary and secondary education for basic capability. In addition, Duncan and Murnane advocate for more attention to research to determine the most effective means to improve elementary and secondary education.[12]

In short, a minimum education—at least completing high school—for the basic capability to enable opportunity to choose among desired outcomes and take responsibility for what is chosen depends to a large extent on ambitious public policies. Obtaining this basic capability cannot be reduced to either individual or family responsibility. To be sure, a few students will fail to translate this basic capability fostered by society into a high school degree, but the current deficit is due largely to a lack of real opportunity rather than to irresponsible behavior by either families or children.

Minimal Provision for Health

Minimal income and a high school education are basic capabilities supporting capability for health, but they alone are insufficient. The SPM and some commentators try to measure healthcare in terms of dollars saved for families alone. The income supplement provided by in-kind healthcare is important, but it fails to consider how access to healthcare and public health enhance the capability for many outcomes and not merely for income savings.

The nation's residents need access to quality healthcare at minimal cost and to public health support to make choices that depend on health, including the choice to nurture their own health and enhance the prospect of a long life. We don't need to insist that good health become a fetish that precludes choices about other, even competing, outcomes. Health and longevity are not the singular goals for a well-lived life. At the very least, some cosmetic health improvements should remain optional and covered by those who want them. Nevertheless, the United States desperately needs universal and reasonably comprehensive[13] high-quality healthcare without significant out-of-pocket costs. We have not obtained that basic capability for fair opportunity for all.

Although healthcare policies vary significantly among nations in the private-public mix, no other developed nation lacks universal health-care at reasonable cost to recipients. The US Congressional Research Service reports that for 2020, 91.4 percent of the US population was covered by some form of public or private health insurance, leaving 8.6 percent of the population (28 million) uninsured. Millions more were underinsured. In 2020, out-of-pocket spending—deductibles, coinsurance, and services not covered—for the publicly and privately insured totaled $389 billion, or 9.9 percent of all healthcare expenditures.[14] These expenditures not only leave many families without minimally adequate resources but also leave them with deficient healthcare because they sacrifice basic healthcare for other family needs, for example, food and shelter. The SPM for 2020 reports that out-of-pocket medical expenses leave an additional five million persons (1.53 percent of the population) below its poverty threshold.[15] These persons cannot cover crucial health needs without great sacrifices in other areas of their nondiscretionary budgets. It is not only a loss of income that detracts from their opportunity but also a capability deficit for basic health.

The extent and quality of health insurance coverage in the United States varies immensely among the states. It also varies by family income levels, education levels, and racial and ethnic groups. The Kaiser Family Foundation reports that 18 percent of Texans were without insurance in 2021. Only Oklahoma approached this level, with 13.8 percent uninsured. Several other states had more than 10 percent of their citizens without health insurance. Some states fared much better, hovering near 5 percent uninsured. Of those states with more than 10 percent of their citizens uninsured, eight of twelve had rejected expanded Medicaid heavily subsidized by the Affordable Care Act.[16] A 2021 "issue brief" from the Office of Healthcare Policy concludes that disparities in healthcare insurance coverage occur for Blacks and Latinx, those with low incomes, and those who live in states without Medicaid expansion.[17] A 2020 US Census Report on healthcare coverage reaches similar findings on insurance coverage for all of these groups and indicates that 28.5 percent of those twenty-six to sixty-four years old who have not graduated from high school remain uninsured, while less than 15 percent of high school graduates are uninsured.[18]

The lack of healthcare insurance is more pronounced among most racial minorities, low-income households, and states that have failed

Chapter 3

to expand Medicaid and aggressively publicized Affordable Care Act insurance. The out-of-pocket annual minimums for individuals and families with ACA insurance are also sufficiently high ($8,700 for individuals and $17,400 for families in 2022) that even this public insurance fails to meet a minimal standard for access to quality healthcare. We see that lack of minimum capability in income and education overlap with but are not identical to less than minimum capability for healthcare. Most recently, with more expansion of the ACA under a new presidential regime and efforts to provide healthcare coverage for COVID patients, we have experienced a slight reduction in uninsured residents. Both lack of private or public insurance and deficient coverage leave persons and families short of the minimum capability needed for fair opportunity. To reiterate: The problem transcends income deficiencies; families and persons lacking easily accessible and affordable healthcare also suffer from a lack of provision for minimal healthcare.

The story of minimal capability for health does not end with the adequacy of comprehensive insurance coverage for healthcare. Our public health practices also lack in some areas: promoting a healthy environment, education about nutrition, exercise, avoiding and treating addictions, security from violence, responding to emergency threats to communities, and protection from communicable diseases.

As we have been reminded by the *Dobbs v. Jackson* overturning of *Roe v. Wade*, a legal environment in which pregnant women can make sound reproductive decisions for themselves and others who depend on them is also crucial. Each of these public health practices, even the latter, varies by degrees. We don't have absolute thresholds beyond which public health is deficient. Furthermore, each of these factors, despite its public provision, can be and often is distributed unevenly by gender, race and ethnicity, geography, and income and education levels. I emphasize that these provisions for health are necessary for capability for real opportunity to make choices for outcomes that persons wish to pursue. They are not merely welcome additions to ease the limits on family budgets or welcome contributions to the common good. They are necessary for fair opportunity.

Remedies

Most studies conclude that the Affordable Care Act has reduced the number and percentage of uninsured in the United States. A 2021 "issue brief" from the Office of Health Policy observes that the number of uninsured in the United States fell from forty million in 2010, the year the ACA was enacted, to twenty-eight million in 2016. Other factors such as the economy are relevant, but the correlation between the ACA and the decline in the uninsured is almost certainly a causal relationship as well. Multiple facets of the ACA, including Medicaid expansion and eligibility for children through twenty-six years of age, contribute to this expansion of access to healthcare.

The ACA has not produced universal comprehensive health insurance coverage. From 2016 until 2020, the number of uninsured increased slightly as the presidential administration at that time tried to repeal the ACA and reduced publicity and incentives to expand coverage. That reversal seems to have dissipated with a new administration and Congress, but there is no clear viable plan to move to universal or near-universal insurance. The ACA neither promises comprehensive coverage for health problems nor covers most out-of-pocket medical expenses. As noted earlier, out-of-pocket costs for a family insured by the ACA may be as high as $17,000—devastating for a family at the poverty threshold of just over $26,000.[19] I reiterate: The lack of capability is not fully measured by the loss of income, because these families will also forgo basic provision for their health.

Improvements in healthcare coverage could come through changes in the ACA that improve subsidies and reduced deductibles and co-pays while appropriately expanding coverage of healthcare treatments. It might be possible to offer a form of Medicare coverage for persons of all ages. These changes are needed to achieve minimum capability of health for all persons. Some persons and families will still choose outcomes short of the pinnacle of health. Others will suffer poor health due to misfortune. However, with universal access and comprehensive coverage at modest out-of-pocket cost, we will approximate fair and equal opportunity for health treatment.

Public health is a distinct matter. Minimum capability in the health sphere also requires structural changes and a culture that supports vibrant public health. Decent public health requires investments in a supportive environment, of course, but it also demands an equitable distribution of environmental protection among racial groups, persons of different income and educational levels, and among different geographical areas. Provisions for a healthy environment have not been evenly distributed, and those who are economically and politically vulnerable have often been subject to onerous environmental hazards. For example, numerous studies show that lead levels are higher for Black persons and poorer populations, especially for children in these groups. Regulation of lead levels is only one example of environmental injustice by race, class, and age. Correcting these injustices that bear on the capability for health and opportunity requires increased data about risks to different groups and sensitivity to group discrepancies in provision for environmental health. It also requires increasing research into detrimental environmental effects and their impact on specific groups. Studies differ regarding the impact of environmental conditions on various groups, but they certainly indicate that some persons cannot control their opportunities for good environmental health.

Investment in a healthier environment is only one area of public health. Similar structural changes are needed to address security related to regulation of weapons of violence and attention to effective security by public officials. Effective public health measures can also reduce addictions, improve nutrition, and diminish other health threats that society alone can address. Some of these, for example, nicotine addiction, are subject to public efforts to change our culture. All of them require constant attention and research to determine what public action will be effective (e.g., recent funding for CDC research into gun regulation).

Public health considerations to diminish climate warming caused by economic policies and practices are vitally important. The multiple effects of climate warming will have a most devasting impact on those with limited resources to respond to flooding, food shortages, and weather disasters. Many—and not only low-income families—will be left without the capability to make choices about the life outcomes they wish to pursue. In this area, research and the publication of research are vitally important to change cultural obstacles to preventive measures, adapt the most effective and economically feasible measures, and help society understand the changing threat to our common life. Additional changes in national and global policies and structure are undoubtedly required.

As noted above, the recent decision in *Dobbs v. Jackson* to overturn *Roe v. Wade* established a momentously important public health context for reproductive health. The changes impinge on the capability of pregnant women to effect opportunities for themselves and family members who depend on them. Whatever one may think about the moral and legal soundness of this decision and the opinion by Justice Alito, there can be no doubt that it profoundly affects opportunities for health, and the effects are not for pregnant women only. The law and rights established or denied also affect the potential life of a fetus, other members of the woman's family, and often friends and partners. The consequences for pregnant women are far greater than for these others except, depending on one's perspective, for the potential life of the fetus. Rational persons differ on the moral and legal status of potential life from the conceptus through the viable fetus, and moral disagreement on this matter diminishes at either extreme on this spectrum.[20] We cannot deny, however, that the opportunities for pregnant women and others for whom they are responsible are severely reduced by highly restrictive laws regarding abortion.

With these considerations in mind, I believe that public health should, with limits when the fetus is viable outside the womb, grant pregnant women a legal right to make these moral decisions for themselves and others.[21] They are the most profoundly affected and in the best position to consider the effects on the lives of others, including potential human life. A reversion to something close to *Roe v. Wade* would show respect for potential human life in the womb while also providing pregnant women the latitude they need to make sound moral decisions that maximize opportunities for many, including themselves. Absent an unlikely revision of *Dobbs*, the means for realizing this balance will have to be state and federal legislation, which is occurring as I write.

I focus extensively upon this matter because it has a momentous effect on capability for opportunities of many persons. To give latitude for mothers to make moral judgments about abortion does not grant them freedom to do whatever they want with their bodies when others are profoundly affected. They should be subject to moral considerations raised by others, but they are the most profoundly affected and in the best position to render a moral judgment. Not every moral judgment should be restricted by civil laws. We may even disagree with the moral judgments of close pregnant friends and associates in this matter, but until the fetus becomes viable, the law should grant the capability for pregnant women to make and execute this judgment. This legal and public health arrangement maximizes opportunity in this highly controversial matter.

None of these remedies to advance minimum capability for healthcare and public health dictate exact structures, laws, policies, and practices, but they offer normative guidance and foci for important research and empirical analysis to improve the current, only partially just, structure. This basic capability cannot guarantee good health. Neither health practices nor accessible quality healthcare precludes bad fortune and risk; however, these structural changes in health and public policy will expand opportunities for many. Individual choices and responsibility will remain factors for actual health. But this fostering of capability will help persons make choices about other health outcomes as well as outcomes in other areas of their lives.

PROVISION FOR COMPREHENSIVE CHILD DEVELOPMENT

Basic capability for children to take responsibility for their own outcomes includes but transcends adequate minimum income, education, or provision for health. We have learned a great deal in recent years about the need for comprehensive nurturing of humans, beginning with conception and continuing through early childhood and beyond. Much of my perspective is informed by *From Neurons to Neighborhoods*.[22] As the name implies, the scientists who prepared this report believe that childhood development must incorporate neurological and other physiological considerations with an environment for social development for children to realize the basic capabilities they need to take responsibility for choosing and executing other outcomes. The authors hold that science has taught us that these factors must be a fully integrated interactive experience for the child. This integrated fostering requires both structural supports for factors such as health, education, and income and interpersonal support in families or a similar intimate and caring group arrangement. Indeed, structural and policy initiatives can promote a propitious environment for interpersonal social and emotional development integrated with brain and other physiological development.

We are increasingly able to assess the basic outcomes of this integrated process by measuring healthy development that is not narrowly confined to access to health, education, and income. We can assess how these factors interact and how they are nurtured by an environment for comprehensive development. This assessment helps us understand how the health, education, and economic inputs foster development for basic capability, as well as the importance of interpersonal contributions to this total development.

Remedies

Clearly, families or surrogates for families have a huge role in providing for this basic and comprehensive development. Provision for real opportunities for children requires that we monitor, assess, and nurture the integrated process if children emerging as adults are to have a real equal opportunity to make choices about other outcomes they wish to pursue. Fair equality of opportunity requires a decent level of this comprehensive nurturing of children of all racial, ethnic, and economic groups. A strictly structural approach to justice or one that neglects how government and structures can help shape communal and interpersonal fostering of capability in settings such as families falls short of what fair equality of opportunity requires. Interpersonal support for children is vital to fostering their capability to choose and achieve the outcomes they desire.

Concern for comprehensive child development as a component of fair equality of opportunity also requires many of the structural reforms discussed in previous sections on minimal provisions for basic capability. It requires special concern for assessment of these integrated structural changes as combined with interactive nurturing in family and family-like settings. We now know more, not just about the importance of providing for income, education, and health but also about how these factors interact with housing, security, and social-emotional support for the child. Good schools and adequate income are important but not enough. Children also need nurturing family relationships. A focus on comprehensive child development demands attention to these integrated factors and the structural and personal initiatives that can advance basic capability for children.

We know that parenting is crucial and that stable two-parent households (not necessarily heterosexual) foster various capabilities for
children in ways that single-parenting or group homes may not. Some
recent studies even show that a lag in educational achievement for young
males may occur, because males in particular benefit from two-parent
households.[23] These data give us reason to promote and support two-
parent households but no reason to denigrate single parents or deny
the possibility of successful parenting in many single-parent homes.
These households need support too. Structural support for families
(for example, the WIC program for nutrition guidance and support for
mothers with limited resources, child tax credits, subsidized childcare,
and pre-kindergarten education) can also stabilize families and support
improved parenting. In addition, structural reforms providing able foster parenting can compensate when parenting in a household falls short.
Certainly, both parental behavior and structural reforms have a role in
fostering basic capability and enhanced opportunities for children. And
structural reforms strengthen families and parenting.

We must transcend the view that fostering development is an isolated
parental responsibility without considering structural support for the
parents—for example, child allowances and subsidies for childcare—
or that structural reforms can substitute for parenting. We must avoid
focusing on structural changes in education policy and the economy as
sufficient without continued attention to and research on the structure
of the family and vital interpersonal relations in the household. We have
learned a great deal about how parenting and other interpersonal supports for child development foster capabilities for children. Substitutes
for parental care are almost always less adequate, although the substitutes also vary in their relative effectiveness: Good foster parents are
preferable to group homes. Fostering basic capability is a complex matter and cannot be reduce to a simple principle or formula.

SATISFYING EMPLOYMENT OR CIVIC
AND POLITICAL ENGAGEMENT

We have considered employment with decent income as necessary for
minimal capability. We have noted the vital importance of opportunities
for available work and/or civic and political participation independent

of compensated employment and other material goods. A well-paying job or position is not the only opportunity persons desire. They often need these opportunities for satisfying and meaningful participation in their communities, even when they have adequate income, education, and healthcare. For some, modestly compensated satisfying work and community participation are in and of themselves sufficient to satisfy well-being. I recall my two Amish aunts, who lived modestly and found satisfaction in cleaning houses and participating in their church. That option will not be adequate for many, but the point is that well-compensated work itself is not always adequate. Work and participation in the community must also be satisfying. Work and participation in civic affairs can contribute to persons' well-being apart from the income derived from them. Martin Luther King Jr. is often cited for choosing the opportunity for civic and political participation at some sacrifice of his own material well-being. Efforts to deny his participation were clearly inconsistent with opportunity to choose the outcomes he desired.

When these forms of participation are unavailable, choices about outcomes are denied. Just any job is not enough without meaningful work. For disadvantaged persons and communities, this lack of opportunity can inhibit or even prevent efforts to address their disadvantages. These outcomes must be considered independently of income because the work and participation may be highly fulfilling outcomes, even as some forms of civic action diminish outcomes for material well-being itself. Martin Luther King Jr.'s work with the Southern Christian Leadership Conference (SCLC) did not produce the best outcomes for his material well-being, but it was a crucial opportunity to pursue personal goals. It was at least tolerated by the structure, although inadequately supported by the FBI and other agencies. A guaranteed income may be sufficient for some persons, but without possibilities for work and community engagement, income may not be adequate. With these possibilities, persons can choose more or less work and civic and political participation.

Remedies

These minimal capabilities suggest various implications for the basic structure of society. First, if technology and productivity enable adequate income without work, persons may not be satisfied unless they retain an opportunity to contribute to the economy and their community by work. Recall again that income is not the only measurement of opportunity for outcomes. Second, our society may have to make possible and encourage a term of community service equivalent to military service. We have had similar opportunities in the past, particularly during Franklin Roosevelt's administration, and many currently recommend a period of mandatory or near-mandatory service. How many of us know family members who found access to well-being through the Peace Corps, HealthCorps, or a government-sponsored domestic volunteer opportunity? Government and nonprofit organizations might promote private-public partnerships, enabling citizens opportunities for participation. Third, laws must be designed to welcome civic and political participation of various kinds so that citizens and residents are fully free to exercise their civic and political rights. Consider, for example, laws that permit formerly incarcerated persons to participate in civic and political activities or that allow persons to pay debts to society by volunteering for the civic good.

Some of these challenges are ever present; others may not be currently acute, but they could be a part of our future. We need to conceive fair opportunity to include outcomes beyond income and education in which persons will be able to find fulfillment through contributions to their society and communities beyond their families.

DECENT HOUSING IN NEIGHBORHOODS

Persons should be free to choose housing in the neighborhoods they desire at market rates unencumbered by restrictions and regulations on the market that impede access by specific classes and races. Substantial evidence indicates that structural factors such as zoning, real estate practices, and ability to obtain loans, combined with the interpersonal behaviors of real estate agents and owners, impede choices about housing and neighborhoods. In some cases, governments and real estate agents have not done enough to eradicate the inertia of historical practices of unjust class and race segregation. In other cases, continuing practices such as zoning for residential neighborhoods and "steering" by real estate agents' loan policies that skirt the law reinforce historical class and race segregation.

We know that these limitations on choosing housing and neighborhoods negatively affect basic capabilities that enable security as well as choices about education, employment, commuting, and civic interaction. We know that children in neighborhoods with concentrated poverty struggle with academic performance and behavior during elementary and secondary education. Without the capability to make choices regarding housing and neighborhoods, families and especially children lack real opportunity for choosing and executing other outcomes. We don't need to contend for subsidies that support choosing whatever housing and neighborhood one desires to oppose policies and practices that impede selecting housing and neighborhoods compatible with these basic capabilities. For example, when zoning practices limit modest-level housing in specific locations, only well-off buyers can choose to reside in those neighborhoods.

In addition to these complex issues of housing in acceptable neighborhoods, the United States suffers from as many as six hundred thousand homeless persons on a given night. Estimates vary. For these individuals and families, housing is an acute problem and neighborhood interaction is virtually nonexistent. Some will contend that homelessness is due to choice or irresponsibility, but from the perspective of this book, these problems manifest a lack of capability for housing with neighborhoods and other supports as long as intervention has any prospect of enabling a choice of decent housing. The obligation of society and individuals to restore capability continues regardless of whether economic deficits, health deficiencies, or irresponsible behavior causes the homelessness—a condition no capable person would choose.

Remedies

We do need to offer adequate public subsidies for housing in mixed income and racial neighborhoods that keep the cost of housing below 30 percent of household income. We need to transform concentrated public housing from low-income housing neighborhoods to mixed-income neighborhoods. We need to change zoning laws that effectively prohibit families with different income levels from residing in a neighborhood. We also need to enforce stronger prohibitions of mortgage and real estate practices that strongly deter mixed-income and interracial housing in neighborhoods. By reducing tax deductions for mortgage interest on expensive housing, we can mitigate concentrations of housing wealth in specific locations. Finally, we should continue to experiment with positive promotion of class and racially integrated housing with programs such as Moving to Opportunity. Moving to Opportunity supports volunteer families moving from areas of concentrated poverty into mixed-income neighborhoods. It has demonstrated some success in promoting psychological and educational benefits, especially for young and female children.

Eradicating or greatly reducing homelessness is a multifaceted task that requires more than provision for temporary housing. Homeless persons suffer lack of minimum capability regarding health, finances, nutrition, a sense of self-dignity, neighborhood interaction, and other aspects of their lives. Housing alone will not resolve the capability deficit that impedes opportunity. Community Solutions, directed by Rosanne Haggerty, a MacArthur Award winner, has developed a multifaceted resolution to homelessness. The approach of Community Solutions shows how addressing the homeless involves a cooperative public/ private coalition in which multiple agencies coordinate efforts.[24] Note that this initiative differs starkly from building temporary tent cities for homeless persons and forcing them outside of populated areas. The latter offers only inadequate shelter bereft of a suitable neighborhood and supports for basic capabilities in other spheres.

Data show that both racial and class segregation in housing continue to exist. Both have disproportionate negative effects for African Americans. They affect social networking, a sense of community, security, and education, in ways that detract from basic capability for opportunity. When structural factors and interpersonal interactions hamper choices pertaining to housing and neighborhoods, persons' and families' different outcomes will be partially determined by restricted opportunity.

MINIMAL SECURITY

For a variety of reasons, often structural, many citizens do not have security from violence that threatens their freedom to choose and execute outcomes. These shortfalls in basic capability for opportunity are disproportionately distributed among demographic groups. There is no doubt that young Black males are subjected to more violence than other demographic groups. This violence includes uneven treatment from police as they execute their professional duties, but that is only part of the threat of violence to specific groups. We have failed to discover the best means to protect some demographic groups, including groups defined by location more than by race or gender, from peer violence. It is difficult to know the extent to which this increased violence may be due to irresponsible behavior by victims, but data clearly show that factors other than individual responsibility are among the principal causes of the violence. These include police conduct but also, probably more important, civic leadership that can prevent and respond to violence, indiscriminate availability of guns and other weapons, and emergency mental health care. Age, race, and gender are principal factors for increased risk of violence, but the group membership does not cause violence, and many preventive factors may reduce its threat to potential victims in these groups.

Persons without a minimum level of education and income and persons who live in neighborhoods of concentrated poverty are subject to increased risk of violence. Blacks in these demographic categories are more vulnerable to violence than other Black persons. Latinx persons are also at higher risk than non-Hispanic Whites but not at as high a risk as Blacks. Whites, as a racial group, are at higher risk than Asian Americans and Pacific Islanders.[25] Some rural or urban areas also experience increased risks. These complex group designations are additionally complicated by considering that different kinds of threats are distributed in different ways among multiple demographic groups. For example, while violence resulting from policing may be more likely for young Black men in some geographical areas, domestic violence may be nearly as likely for some lower socioeconomic status (SES) Whites. Since these different threats are not principally matters of individual irresponsibility, we need to learn much more about likely threats to different demographic groups to adequately address basic capability for fair opportunity.

Remedies

An effort to enhance basic capability by reducing threats of violence must begin with a more precise understanding of which groups are most vulnerable and the sources of violence to which they are vulnerable. Studies demonstrate that young African American males are more likely to experience violence resulting from unnecessarily aggressive—sometimes even malicious or intentional—police violence, but this demographic group is also subject to neighborhood violence and violence committed during criminal activity. In addition, other groups—for example, lower SES Whites in some geographical areas—are subject to violence resulting from excessive police action or to domestic violence. What groups are most subject to violence within schools by single or a small group of perpetrators or to other kinds of mass violence using guns of various kinds?

We need more empirical research from the CDC (Centers for Disease Control and Prevention), educational institutions, and nonprofits funded by public money to provide knowledge regarding the role of gun regulations, school safety, and mental health. The issue here is not simply whether individual responsibility by persons contributes—it does, of course—but also whether we can limit other contributing causes, for example, gun violence or inattention to bad behavior in schools and parenting that fails to protect children from violence.

Plausible remedies can follow from this evidence. If we know there is danger to lives, especially the lives of children and racial or ethnic groups, due to access to specific weapons that are not usable for self-defense or even for hunting, that information provides a way forward to curtail violence with minimal or no negative consequences. We need better data regarding reduced risked associated with specific gun regulations relative to other consequences of gun regulations, such as curtailing the capacity for self-defense and the freedom to hunt. Persons' rights to guns for pleasure or target practice are not equivalent to their rights to guns for self-defense or hunting. In some cases, individual rights may be curtailed with minimal harm to the rights holder who benefits minimally—for example, the joy of owning a gun—when the consequences of the legal protection may threaten others with grave harm. Research into the consequences of legal rights to own and use guns is a public health matter bearing on fair equality of opportunity. Some groups may be denied minimal capability to choose how to avoid security risks.

With better public health data regarding violence, we can more effectively address root causes, for example, ineffective and overly aggressive policing, improperly focused policing, inadequate social work and therapeutic help, insufficient gun regulation (perhaps especially for handgun possession in public settings), inadequate security at some institutions (especially schools), inadequate responses to mental health emergencies, and neighborhood class and race segregation. Surely, reforms in policing and judicial practices—for example, no-knock warrants—that go beyond mere stricter enforcement against irresponsible police behavior are needed. Hiring and training practices and monitoring police behavior are all important. We need new efforts by local jurisdictions as well as scrutiny by state and federal agencies to scrutinize, support, and sometimes demand local reforms. These efforts are necessary to provide basic capability for the opportunity to make choices about outcomes that individuals can execute. Without them, fully fair equality of opportunity is impossible. Individuals are vulnerable to fates they do not choose for themselves.

PRELIMINARY CONCLUSIONS
REGARDING MINIMUM CAPABILITY

Positive steps by society can help provide minimum income levels and education, basic universal health care and public health, comprehensive child development, satisfying work and civic participation, decent housing and neighborhoods, and reasonable security from violence. These are structural requirements for fair equality of opportunity. Fostering these capabilities for opportunity also requires interactions among individuals in households and other settings. Fair opportunity cannot be left to the responsibility to avoid prejudices judging qualifications or to enforcement prohibiting this unjust discrimination. Both structural and interpersonal positive efforts to nurture minimum capability for opportunity are necessary. Fair equality of opportunity requires both changes in structures that coerce and changes in interpersonal behavior in various contexts.

This minimal basic capability for real opportunity is essential for fair equality of opportunity, but it falls far short of fully just opportunity.

OVERCOMING FATE AND RENEWING
BASIC CAPABILITY

What more is needed? Persons lacking opportunity due to previous detrimental behavior or misfortune, even when they are irresponsible,[26] should be provided capability to recover from limitations such as disabilities in mental or physical health, addiction, or negative vestiges of incarceration. This may include the disruptive psychological vestiges of their own wrongdoing. However, it should be clear by now that irresponsible behavior is not the only reason for these misfortunes.

They often result from bad luck or injustices in the provision for fair opportunity. As Bruce Western, professor of sociology and criminal justice at Harvard University, has noted in several publications, addiction and incarceration are not always easily traceable to irresponsible behavior, although irresponsibility can have a role too.[27] Note that behavior is not binary between responsible and irresponsible; often, our behavior falls into a range between responsible and irresponsible. The destructive consequences of a person's irresponsible behavior may be far more detrimental to that person than whatever their irresponsible behavior contributed. Think of differences between an upper-middle-class person driving while partly intoxicated in their own neighborhood and a poor person or person of color driving while intoxicated in that same middle-class neighborhood. Accountability for irresponsible behavior is always complicated. There is no formula for judgment and punishment that perfectly fits the behavior, and the response to personal irresponsibility varies among persons. Moreover, we are sometimes fortunate that our irresponsible behavior is not seriously detrimental. Who among us has driven recklessly or while slightly intoxicated without harm to ourselves or others? Just lucky!

Whether or not persons have some responsibility for their lost basic capability, imprisoned and addicted persons, along with recently disabled persons, should be provided with good nutrition, healthcare, and education and other supports as plateaus to foster basic capability for functioning. The capability for renewal may also have to be nurtured by fostering the social bases of self-respect, including structures and interpersonal interactions that may require appropriate forgiveness. In some cases, diminishing the debilitating vestiges of guilt will require expressions of forgiveness by those who have been injured (not merely by society in general). Those expressions may be facilitated by institutional structures but often entail meaningful interpersonal interaction. These acts of fostering what some might call "unearned" or "undeserved" capability are warranted by appropriate understandings of grace, merit, and desert, as previously discussed. They may include efficacious negative judgments motivated by a desire and intention to facilitate contrition, redemption, and renewed opportunities. Well-targeted and well-timed judgments can spur us to make appropriate corrections. On these occasions, judgments are, somewhat ironically, also acts of grace for us. They are generous and seemingly unmerited efforts to redeem irresponsible behaviors. Choices about and execution of outcomes should never be left entirely to the responsibility of the person needing renewal of basic capability. All of us need to experience judgment by others and then, when we are ready, forgiveness or compassionate support in order to advance new outcomes beyond our shortcomings.

For persons who have been disabled, renewal may require a combination of practices to overcome a disability, policies to adjust circumstances that prevent functioning with a disability, and interpersonal expressions of respect that facilitate renewed confidence.[28]

Fostering basic minimal capability for real opportunity is not restricted to some initial provision by a basic structure and families and associates. The frequently expressed view that equal opportunity is achieved by getting all citizens to the same starting line is grossly inadequate. Justice in relation to basic capability for real opportunity demands vigilance in sustaining capability and renewing lost capabilities for functioning. For example, as aging diminishes some capabilities, structural and interpersonal adjustments are necessary to foster the capability for fair equality of opportunity.

Individuals should not be left solely responsible for choosing and executing outcomes beyond some initial minimum functioning. They need self-respect and the respect from others that may require forgiveness in some cases and special care for fostering confidence and dissipating self-doubt in other cases. These achievements require both interpersonal efforts from family, friends, and associates and structural changes, such as accessible and subsidized mental health therapy, provision for developing new skills, or collectively initiated opportunities—for example, provision for employment or civic participation to overcome the vestiges of detrimental behavior. Emphasis on a starting-line metaphor or on individual responsibility ignores capability deficits that persons cannot overcome without nurturing from other persons and institutions at multiple junctures in their lives. The image of equal opportunity as a onetime offer for individuals when it needs renewal and sustaining of opportunity completely misses the reality of capability for choices and executing them responsibly.

Remedies

Fostering renewed and updated capability requires a myriad of structural arrangements. Persons who encounter physical and mental disabilities require provision for comprehensive therapy and mental health services, including long-term counseling when needed, without significant out-of-pocket costs. The CDC reports that 26 percent of US adults have some type of disability. Most of these adults can function satisfactorily and even at a high level with adequate support, and they also foster capability for others. The prodigious task of fostering basic capability for this large number of citizens also requires interpersonal support from family, friends, and groups. It cannot be left to structural arrangements alone, although structures like the CDC can encourage, inform, and guide interpersonal support.

The astoundingly high incarceration rates in the United States are well-known, as well as the disproportionate imprisonment of persons of color—especially young African American males. Bruce Western and his colleagues found that by the turn of the millennium, nearly 60 percent of young Black males without a high school education had spent some time in prison. Equally astounding, Black men in their early thirties in 1999 were more likely by substantial margins to have been in prison than to have been in the military or hold a bachelor's degree. The point is not that more Black men should get a college degree to avoid prison, but that a high percentage of Black men end up in prison rather than achieving outcomes for which they should be capable. This cohort faces a high probability of incarceration. Perhaps less well known, more than 11 percent of approximately thirty-year-old high school drop-out White males had spent time in prison by 2000. I hasten to add two further observations: The increased imprisonment in 2000 for approximately thirty-year-old males compared to 1979 was nearly triple for White males and more than triple for Black males.[29] Moreover, the lack of a high school education is an important factor (beyond gender, race, and age) for predicting high levels of incarceration.

Although these data about the magnitude of imprisonment are astounding, the deleterious effects on basic capability resulting from imprisonment, especially for young males, is also telling and probably less widely appreciated.

First, consider the impact on families in formation before the parents are thirty. Will these mostly young men be able to maintain contact with children for which they almost always care and have primary responsibility—and with spouses or partners? Keep in mind that family support is a crucial ingredient for basic capability, especially for children.

Second, healthcare and provision for health for imprisoned persons is notoriously inadequate, especially for addiction and depression, which are common among young, incarcerated persons.

Third, continuing education and preparation for participation in the economy and society are difficult during imprisonment. These capabilities need special emphasis while persons are incarcerated and immediately afterward.

Fourth, formerly incarcerated persons are at a huge disadvantage in the job market simply because of the résumés they must submit. They need some sort of protection from prejudices against persons who have been imprisoned, for example, banning a box requiring indication of a misdemeanor or felony with the initial application for employment. These reporting requirements may be nearly as unfairly discriminatory in relation to true qualifications as outright discrimination based on race or gender. Jamie Dimon (CEO of JPMorgan Chase) writes in a recent opinion column in the *New York Times* about the difficulty and cost of expunging criminal records and the need for proactive mentoring that incarcerated persons miss and that are needed to facilitate their employment.[30]

Fifth, laws that prohibit convicted persons from receiving public assistance—in-kind and cash—are devastating for those who have few resources other than help from family and friends after incarceration. Addicted persons forced to linger in prison without therapy are especially disadvantaged when the balance of evidence shows that addiction therapy for persons functioning in society is more likely to ameliorate addictions than continued imprisonment. This failure to foster renewed capability has become racially discriminatory in the United States, although it also disadvantages young males (and females in smaller numbers) of many races who lack a minimum education.

Finally, persons who have completed a sentence need to be returned to full citizenship—including being able to vote and participate in politics—to feel fully incorporated into their society and to lobby for restructuring incarceration policy. Impediments to full citizenship and civic participation after incarcerations do not serve as deterrents or appropriate retributive justice. Making these privileges of citizenship contingent on paying legal debts to the criminal justice system undermines the opportunity to participate in society.

None of these proffered remedies includes reducing overly long sentences, although these sentences may be unnecessary for deterrence and a problem in many cases. Nevertheless, incarceration is sometimes necessary as a deterrent or simply to keep dangerous persons from participating in society. Empirical data about recidivism and crimes by released prisoners are important for determining the need for sentence length.

The key element in the remedies proposed here is not shortening sentences, although that may be warranted on grounds of justice. The key feature of these remedies is to enable opportunities most likely to lead to renewed functioning in society for persons leaving incarceration.

In sum, these sweeping changes—primarily structural—could do much to restore the basic minimal capability for choosing and pursuing desirable outcomes after serious disruptions in life opportunities. The issue here is not merely one of mercy and forgiveness, although we probably need more of both. The issue calls for empirical data about what works in addition to a normative commitment to real opportunity for all. We should be concerned about what policies and practices are most likely to restore formerly incarcerated persons to functioning citizenship and civic and family life. Capability for opportunity still requires choices and execution of those choices for formerly incarcerated persons.

Not all need for renewing capability arises from unexpected or unpredictable events. In addition, capability deficits may occur during the aging process. Results of aging are not contingent on dramatic unfortunate events. The effects of age require changes in what is needed to foster capability. Aging persons become dependent on special and expanded healthcare and on public health to enable basic functioning in executing intellectual and social development. These capabilities may be fostered by in-home healthcare, social gatherings, information and assistance for nutritional needs, and support for civic involvement. Obviously, the requirements differ for different persons and families and may demand changes in structure such as Medicare for in-home care and provision for interpersonal interactions among family members and members of the larger community. These capabilities enable aging persons to make new choices about the changing outcomes they desire for themselves.

Policies and practices required for minimal basic capability to choose and pursue outcomes are clearly not limited to prohibiting discriminatory prejudices regarding qualifications for positions. The discussions address structural changes and interpersonal behavior necessary to foster opportunity, including minimal income and education and provision for minimal health—enabling persons and groups to have the opportunity for choosing varied outcomes beyond the minimal. In addition, conditions for comprehensive child development, including stable families and key support for young children, require positive action by society and by individuals. Without both structural and interpersonal fostering of capabilities, children will lack fair opportunity to make their own choices about well-being. Society must also nurture and support the prospect for satisfying work and civic service and political engagement under reasonable conditions.

Material well-being alone is insufficient if persons are unable choose to contribute to one another and society. These basic capabilities depend on decent housing in supportive neighborhoods with security from violence and the threat of harm from any quarter. Again, these provisions require positive actions by enacting laws and policies—for example, housing subsidies, zoning and tax laws, a fair policing and criminal justice system—to ensure opportunity for choosing and pursuing outcomes. Without these provisions, income, education, healthcare, and available work will not be possible or sufficient for persons to choose and pursue their desired outcomes. These desired outcomes may range from more challenging work, desirable housing, advanced education, or other elements of well-being, such as family life, civic participation, or leisure time.

Finally—often neglected and perhaps most crucial—the many persons who have suffered misfortune or faltered in some way, whether or not they are partially responsible, often lack the basic minimal capability to recapture a level of fair opportunity to choose and pursue outcomes they desire. I accentuate that fair opportunity is not merely bringing persons to a one-time equal chance for some achievement at a starting line. Neither is it providing for all persons an equal set of outcomes without regard to their responsible action. It is a sustained process of fostering and renewing the basic capability for real opportunities and responsibility for outcomes persons desire.

Individual responsibility for choosing among and executing different outcomes for full well-being and a satisfying life does not come into play until these basic capabilities are provided for each person. But provision of minimal basic capability does not exhaust the requirements for fair equality of opportunity.

OUTCOMES BEYOND BASIC CAPABILITY

Fair equality of opportunity also demands that individuals and associations of like-minded persons have an opportunity to advance their desires and well-being beyond these minimal outcomes. These advanced outcomes beyond the minimum will differ according to the goals persons choose to pursue and take responsibility to execute. Some will choose and pursue more income and some additional education. Others will prefer other and different outcomes both within education and employment opportunities and in other areas, for example, leisure time, civic involvement, or family time.

Some will also work more diligently to continue achieving outcomes of which they are capable. Some will work to access and perform well at the most prestigious and elite higher education institutions and the most demanding jobs. Others will work hard to become civic or political leaders such as Martin Luther King Jr., Bill Clinton, the Bushes, Barack Obama, and Kamala Harris.

Some might choose a four-year college major in the liberal arts and others in the sciences. Some might choose training in welding beyond high school and show little interest in higher education. Some might choose to earn income in nonprofits serving community needs; others in finance, law, or medicine. Some may choose more leisure time with less work and income or more time with family members, including children, while curtailing work and income. Some may curtail their most ambitious goals in midlife. We cannot measure equality of opportunity based on these outcomes alone.

That some persons and families have more income or highly prestigious jobs does not, in and of itself, indicate greater opportunity—or higher achievement and well-being. The outcomes should be chosen and achieved by responsible behavior, not expected or imposed on persons. We should not assume that individuals who are not high-level professionals but provide services for community nonprofits, for example, are denied opportunity or fail to achieve equal—maybe even greater—well-being. Too many accounts of opportunity and achievement—some of them assuming that they are based on revealing data—equate opportunity, success, or both with income levels, education levels, or some other designated quantitative accomplishment.

With this understanding of equal opportunity, we should not make the mistake of linking greater income or education with merit. Adrian Wooldridge (see chapter 1, note 2) makes this common mistake. In his view, the triumph of merit means that those with the greatest innate talent, usually equated with innate intelligence measured by something akin to IQ, can be determined by income and education levels as long as achievements are not unjustly skewed by inherited income, social prestige, or ancestorial advantages. Wooldridge is far too sophisticated to assume that all income and education outcomes in the modern world are based on merit, but he does believe that in the most just societies, these outcomes indicate greater opportunity and economic efficiency because qualifications are allowed to result in inequalities of income and education.

This mistaken view equates specific outcomes with merit and wrongly conceives merit as innate intelligence, although Woolridge clearly distinguishes this intelligence from the social standing into which persons are born. He also mistakenly accentuates economic efficiency as a common good. That view differs sharply from respect for fair and equal opportunity as understood in this book. If we recognize the importance of fostering capability for real opportunity to choose and achieve, merit cannot be equated with any particular set of unequal outcomes. Just but unearned structural accommodations that foster capability of choice and achievement precede merit. When persons are granted capability for choosing and achievement, merit is not the principal relevant factor in their outcomes; real opportunity—that is, the capability to choose outcomes and to *become* meritorious—is. Merit is secondary. It follows capabilities fostered by others and choice about preferred outcomes.

It follows that different outcomes could result from a lack of capability and opportunity, from different choices about what is valuable, or perhaps by irresponsible execution in pursuing desires one is capable of achieving. How then do we know if persons with varied and unequal outcomes have been denied opportunity, pursued different outcomes they have chosen, or failed to take responsibility for outcomes they desired? Both anecdotal and quantitative data help here.

Freedom to Choose Outcomes for Well-Being

First, we should question the commonplace view that persons who receive a higher income and achieve advanced educational degrees at elite institutions are more successful in achieving the outcomes they desired. Some persons choose lower income employment that they enjoy more or that is more satisfying in what it accomplishes. Others may choose greater relaxation and leisure with employment that compensates less. Some may prefer on-the-job training, technical training, or an associate degree in community college over four years or more of higher education. Advanced degrees do not necessarily indicate greater opportunity, higher achievement, or greater well-being.

Increases in household income, although modest over the last two decades, and in the number of US residents seeking college and advanced degrees make it apparent that more income and education are desirable for many. However, not all persons who receive a smaller income or less standard education beyond high school are denied fair opportunities or are irresponsible. Some may simply choose different outcomes.

Evidence for Lack of Fair Opportunity in Outcomes

Others are no doubt denied fair opportunity. How do we identify these persons?

First, when a disproportionate number of persons from racial groups, geographical areas, lower socioeconomic status, and among females or disabled persons do not have outcomes proportionate to other groups, we can be relatively confident that the outcomes do not result from individual irresponsibility or personal choices. We have little reason to believe a high proportion of individuals from these groups desire or deserve less income or education than those from other groups. Subcultural factors may explain some of these differences, but we should be suspicious of those factors; they are often sustained by structural realities that maintain unequal opportunity for choice. They go under the guise of choices rooted in subcultural differences but often reflect deeper unequal opportunities. For example, expectations about which gender should provide the bulk of childcare and policies that leave households to provide their own childcare and parental leave after birth militate against women choosing employment or other demanding work outside the home.

Persons with disabilities often cannot have identical capabilities among themselves or with others. They may adjust their choices about education and employment to accommodate these differing capabilities. Nevertheless, these fated differences should not, in most cases, limit advancement in income or in some type of education. Disabilities inevitably preclude some professional careers—my damaged eyesight prohibited me from choosing baseball as a career no matter how much I aspired to be like Ernie Banks—and some kinds of education. Still, roughly equal careers and education are possible without identical capability. In most cases, disabilities should not result in significant differences in income or educational attainment, even if the means of earning income and the kind of education may be altered. If speaking disabilities render a career in newscasting and a degree in public speaking impossible, the person can still aim for a high-income position and a reputable college degree. Some disabilities prohibit specific types of education—for example, in language or mathematics—without reducing possibilities for other types of education at a high level. In such cases, identical capability is not possible, but equal capability is.[31]

DISTRIBUTION OF MEDIAN INCOME

What evidence demonstrates a lack of opportunity to attain income beyond the minimum level? What if median income differs significantly among different groups with no adequate explanation for this inequality?

For instance, we know from the US Census Bureau that median income for Blacks in 2020 was estimated at $45,870, $55,321 for Hispanics, and $74,912 for Whites. (It was markedly higher for Asians.) A 2021 Statista report indicates a median income for disabled persons in 2019 of $40,360 as compared to $48,406 for those without disabilities.[32] Without drawing specific conclusions about the causes of unequal opportunity, we can be confident that a larger portion of Black, Hispanic, and disabled persons do not choose to reject higher incomes or conduct their economic lives irresponsibly. Some individuals in these groups may make a choice for different income outcomes, but not a much larger proportion than for other groups. What adequately explains these data? One possibility is that US society fails to provide Blacks, Hispanics, and (in many cases) disabled persons with minimum basic capabilities in the same proportions that it provides these minimum basic capabilities for groups such as Whites and Asians, who have higher median incomes on average. Hence the disadvantaged groups are unable in the same proportions to choose and pursue greater income as their preferred outcome. They do not, as groups, have the same opportunities for higher levels of income.

Latinx immigrants may be distinct, because evidence suggests that their lower income as a group results partly from their rapidly increasing numbers and is modified by higher mobility from one generation to the next. A recent empirical study of immigration demonstrates that second-generation immigrants have always been more upwardly mobile (as measured by income) than persons from longtime US families. (This second-generation mobility does not mean that new immigrants have equal capability and opportunity as established citizens, but they are more mobile as a group.) Since Latinx immigrants are currently predominant, this mobility is pronounced among them. Perhaps the relatively low median income among Latinx persons is attributable to their recent arrival rather than long-term unequal capability to earn a median income. This evidence also dispels a widely held view that

Latinx immigrants undermine the US economy by failing to contribute and pay taxes for the services they use.[33]

DISTRIBUTION OF HIGHER
EDUCATION DEGREES

We also have conclusive evidence for unequal attainment in education that cannot be explained by individual choices or irresponsible pursuit of desired outcomes.

The Census Bureau informs us that in 2015, 36.2 percent of twenty-five-year-old Whites had received a bachelor's degree compared to 22.5 percent of Blacks and 15.5 percent of Hispanics. (Asians are again the outlier, with 53.9 percent of twenty-five-year-old Asians holding a bachelor's degree in 2015.) As with median income data, the Hispanic numbers are somewhat skewed by immigration that allows for high levels of mobility from the first generation to the next. Only 16.7 percent of twenty-five-year-old persons with disabilities had received a bachelor's degree in 2015 compared with 34.9 percent of those without disabilities.[34]

Once again, disproportions in higher education degrees among these groups can hardly be explained by individual choice or greater irresponsible execution of desires among these different groups. As with disproportionate income levels, disproportion in advanced education degrees among these groups can be explained, at least in part, as due to societal structures not providing some groups in equal proportions with minimum basic capability to choose and execute choices for advanced education.

Let's again consider lack of minimum basic capability for these groups that do not receive a median income or colleges degrees in proportion to others. It may be that the disproportionality in higher income and levels of education is explained, at least in part, by disproportion fostering of basic minimal capability among identifiable groups.

LACK OF BASIC CAPABILITY AS A
CAUSE OF DISPROPORTIONATE
OUTCOMES AT HIGHER LEVELS

The data are revealing. The Census Bureau reports that for 2016, 93.3 percent of Whites, 87 percent of Blacks, and 66.7 percent of Hispanics twenty-five and older graduated from high school. (Asians graduated from high school at a slightly lower rate than Whites.[35]) Disabled persons at age twenty-five were less than 80 percent likely to hold a high school degree compared to nearly 90 percent of those without a disability.[36] These discrepancies are significant, especially in light of likely additional discrepancies in the quality of neighborhoods and high school education among these different groups.

The proportion of some groups who live at or below the income poverty level as measured by both the US official rate and the SPM also indicate that some groups are disproportionately denied the basic capability to make choices about the income levels they would prefer to attain. The official poverty measure (below $13,788 for a single household head and approximately $27,740 for a four-person household in 2021) shows that 19.5 percent of Blacks and 17.1 percent of Hispanics lived in households below the poverty threshold compared to just over 9.9 percent of Whites. A similar disproportionality occurs for disabled persons, of whom 24.9 percent were officially poor in 2021 by US standards. According to the SPM, 11.3 percent of Blacks and 11.2 percent of Hispanics lived below its poverty threshold compared to a markedly lower rate of poverty of 5.7 percent for Whites. Unsurprisingly, a more modest 15.8 percent of disabled persons were considered poor according to the SPM.[37] In sum, a significantly higher proportion of disabled persons live in impoverished households according to both measurements.

Despite somewhat different poverty thresholds and measurements, these two ways of calculating poverty indicate a level of income below the minimum required for the basic capability for real opportunity for Blacks, Hispanics, and disabled persons. The measurements for Native Americans are even more disproportionally below minimum income. We should note that a significant percentage of Whites and Asians also lack these minimum income levels. They are not spared commensurate restrictions on opportunity. Until 2021, a significantly higher percentage of children in all groups lived in households below both the OFM and SPM thresholds, exacerbating the dilatory effects of exceedingly low income on opportunity.[38]

Still, lack of minimum education and income alone do not adequately explain group differences in median income and advanced education. Beyond differences in poverty level income and the quantity and quality of minimal education, we should acknowledge unequal access to healthcare and provision for public health, and especially the huge discrepancy in incarceration for young Black men. The Kaiser Family Foundation reports the uninsured rate for healthcare among Whites and Asians in the 7 percent range, whereas it is over 11 percent for Blacks and over 20 percent for Hispanics and Native Americans. The provision for public health, especially protection from environmental hazards, is also disproportionate among the races. Environmental injustice occurs, in part, due to racially concentrated housing in impoverished neighborhoods. Public health practices, whether civic or governmental, fail to protect the environment in disadvantaged neighborhoods. The effect on education due to incarceration may be even more pronounced than the effects of low income, other causes of inadequate minimum education, and minimum public health. Combined, these differences in structural support for different racial and ethnic groups explain much of the discrepancy in the median income level and advanced education degrees among the groups. In addition to effects on racial groups, these factors disproportionately affect working-class and geographically isolated families in all racial groups.

Disability as a factor is somewhat different for several reasons. As previously noted, it may not be possible to bring all disabled persons to a fully equal minimum capability due to the nature of some disabilities, for example, severe autism or Down syndrome. Furthermore, differences in the equal basic capabilities for a variety of disabled persons may lead to different choices for the types of jobs and education they pursue. We can imagine, even without clear verifying data, that persons with principally physical disabilities might be more likely to choose advanced education degrees rather than physically demanding labor that does not require advanced education. Finally, income subsidies for disabled persons, welcomed to diminish income poverty, may be administered in a way that discourages—or at least does not support—the motive to work and contribute to society independent of income needs. For example, supplemental security income (SSI) may signal mistakenly and unnecessarily that recipients are incapable of advanced education or meaningful work. There is more to how income subsidies incentivize and disincentivize work and employment than the income itself. There is also the way in which it is administered to engender self-respect and confidence. For many disabled persons, opportunities to contribute to their communities are as important as income or prestige. Policies that either discourage or don't encourage such opportunities are as detrimental to real opportunity as policies that militate against higher income or more advanced education.

What about differences among Asians *and other groups*? Here, sustained cultural factors—not among Asians in general—but of Asians who have immigrated to the United States may help explain higher income and advanced education consistent with an even slightly lower high school graduation rate than Whites. Whereas many Hispanic immigrants are fleeing poverty, Asian immigrants are often, but not uniformly, from higher income and advanced educational backgrounds and seeking even higher economic status. We should not be surprised by their higher median income levels and advanced education beyond other groups, which is not inconsistent with continuing individual prejudice and anger toward some Asians, especially East Asians, during the recent COVID-19 crisis.

Fair opportunity for a group can coexist with significant outlashing by individuals toward persons in the group. Some individual White nationalists lash out against Jews or African Americans who achieve outcomes commensurate with the opportunities available to them. This kind of individual hateful lashing out is not the same as structural injustice toward these groups. Recall again that fair equality of opportunity depends on individual attitudes and behavior as well as the structure of society. These individual attitudes and behavior would not be revealed in overall data about income and education. They would, nonetheless, leave some Asians and Jews with diminished capability to participate in interactions among fellow citizens.

Data and discrepancies in basic capabilities for *gender* differ from other groups. Women receive less income and are more impoverished than males in the United States; however, they graduate from high school and college at a higher rate than males, and various data bases show the gap in educational attainment favoring women is growing.

By contrast, median earnings for women in 2022 were, according to the Pew Research Center, 82 percent of male earnings, an earnings gap that has only gradually dissipated in recent years.[39] Is the continued decisive, albeit reduced, difference in earnings conclusive evidence for unequal opportunities?

There are complicating factors. Clearly, unequal minimum basic capability in education does not explain the differences; incarceration and addiction rates do not explain the earnings differential either. Incarceration rates would seem to indicate even less choice for men. What about differences in men's and women's minimal income? Women live in poverty households at a greater rate than men: In 2019, 11.5 percent of females, compared with 9.4 percent of males, lived in households below the poverty threshold and 12.4 percent of females and 11.1 percent of males lived below the SPM threshold. (The difference in the gap between these two poverty rates may be significant for remedies to the unfair opportunity in this case. See below.)

Recall that the SPM threshold is slightly higher and measures resources slightly differently from cash income alone, but both measures use a threshold minimum far below the median income of households. These differences in below-minimum income for basic capability to choose and execute outcomes are significant. They help explain the lower capability of women to choose higher income as desirable for well-being for themselves and their families. The minimum income differentials are even more significant considering that more single-parent families (with proportionally much lower income households and other challenges) are headed by females.

Lack of minimum income (including in-kind support) is a factor for the lower median income of women, but we might still plausibly attribute some of the lower median income of women to a choice to seek different outcomes with more desire for childbearing and child-rearing than maximizing income. That sort of choice is fully rational and would not indicate diminished fair opportunity apart from two qualifications.

First, the choice, even for childbearing, may not be antithetical with maximizing income over time. Second the "choice" may be dictated by subcultural factors that are influenced by opportunity-limiting structural factors, such as provision for public support of paid maternity leave, subsidized daycare, and early education. Some data, especially anecdotal data, strongly suggest that structural changes such as paid parental leave, income allowances for children, and childcare subsidies alter circumstances and expand choices for women relative to employment and childbearing and child-rearing. They may even provide opportunity for choices that some women could not have imagined because they are constrained by a lack of capability due to these structural constraints.

We are entering complicated territory here, because women, due to biologically rooted or freely selected subcultural preferences, may choose time devoted to childbearing and child rearing over maximizing income through employment. To limit that choice or deny its authenticity and legitimacy would also restrict fair equality of opportunity, as I have noted from the outset. Women should be able to make that choice, assuming they have the capability to choose otherwise. That is why our determination of fair opportunity relative to income outcomes requires qualitative observations and anecdotal evidence as well as quantitative data. On occasion, some groups may freely disproportionately choose not to maximize an outcome that others, including some women, may assume preferable for everyone. We must listen carefully to what mothers—and fathers, who in some cases prefer child-rearing to more income—have to say about themselves and their presumed "choices."[40]

We have sufficient quantitative and qualitative evidence to conclude that race- and ethnic-based differentials in median income and education at the undergraduate college level and higher are at least partly attributable to lack of capability for the opportunity to make choices about desirable levels of income and education. These and other restrictions on opportunity—limited access to healthcare, housing in suitable neighborhoods, and treatment for addiction and incarceration policies—are structural and largely independent of prejudicial discrimination regarding qualifications for positions. For these groups, deficits in fostering a basic minimal capability definitely curtail fair equality of opportunity. Additionally, failure to provide minimum capability for opportunity in the form of policies such as paid parental leave, subsidized childcare, or provision for preschool education also limits, although in a different way, opportunity for many females.

Remedies

Policies such as child allowances, increased minimum wage, earned income tax credits, subsidized pre-kindergarten education, expanded access to healthcare, and improved neighborhood housing will foster basic capability for lower SES members of all racial and ethnic groups. Nonetheless, due to the disproportionate numbers of Black, Latinx (especially recent immigrants), and Native Americans who lack minimum basic capability, expansion of fair opportunity through these policies will be proportionally greater for these demographic groups. In addition, reforming incarceration policy and detrimental ingrained practices in some elementary and high schools affect opportunities disproportionately for Black young men—and to some extent for young White men. Housing and neighborhood racial segregation also have racially differential consequences.

This special attention to how structures affect basic capability and opportunity for persons of different races is part of what critical race theory seeks to reveal, although I believe identifying specific laws and practices is more appropriate for understanding and remedying race-based lack of fair opportunity than is a generalized theory. "Systematic racism" does not tell us much; specific zoning laws or environmental injustices that jeopardize the health of Black neighborhoods and disproportionate suspension of Black children in schools provide foci for effective remedies. These observations reiterate a major theme in this book: Fair opportunity requires positive steps to augment capability; prohibiting prejudicial judgments about qualifications for a position or appointment is not sufficient. Neither are theories that proffer abstract charges of generalized racism, sexism, or class conflict. We need specific structural changes to foster equal capability for choice and functioning.

Solutions to the injustice of unfair opportunity for disabled persons and the hope for eradicating unfair opportunity for disabled persons differ—and are perhaps more complicated. The common factor for disability and race is the historically disproportionate lack of attention to fostering minimal basic capability. For disabled persons, the failure includes insufficient income and education due to slow progress in treating correctable disabilities and adjusting the circumstances of the workplace and education to accommodate the distinctive capabilities of disabled persons. Direct provision of income and open access to education alone are insufficient. We must apply well-established adjustments for specific disabilities. We now know about—and to some extent have effected—changes that allow for more nearly equal, even though not identical, capabilities for disabled persons. The established adjustments must be universally applied to foster minimal capability for disabled persons.

This does not mean that minimal basic capability can be provided for every disabled person. As noted earlier, some disabilities are sufficiently recalcitrant that adjustments to provide minimal and equal basic capabilities cannot be provided, at least without costs that deny equal capabilities to many others. This latter qualification is not a concession for the sake of overall economic efficiency and welfare. We should accept some reduction in collective economic welfare to respect the dignity of all humans. The limits on investments to achieve equal capability for some disabled persons occur because such investment can diminish opportunity for many others. These kinds of cost/benefit considerations are, of course, never a reason for denying even the most severely disabled person opportunities for some choices—for example, employment and participation in civic events—even when equal basic capability with others is not possible.

Fair opportunity for disabled persons also requires research to advance knowledge of what can be done to foster capability for persons with various disabilities and vigilance in adjusting circumstances that undermine capability for persons with disabilities. Consider the expanded opportunities resulting from technology for improving sight and hearing and how hearing and vision devices have enabled enhanced choices for many persons. Consider how discoveries into the causes of and therapy for disabilities such as autism, attention deficit disorder, and various addictions have helped augment capabilities for persons with these disabilities. Equally important, these advances have changed our cultural response to persons manifesting these disorders. Without continuing to advance knowledge of what can be done and making commensurate structural changes, claims to eradicate prejudices regarding the qualifications of disabled persons are grossly inadequate. Once again, we need to foster capability for qualifications rather than merely avoiding prejudices against disabled persons.

Remedies for unfairness in opportunities for *women* present yet another challenge. Minimum education is not a problem. However, the gap in median income between males and females is not—in most cases—a matter of women's choices. The gap often results from the failure of society to foster minimum basic capabilities due to lack of minimum income and a lack of in-kind support that could make both income through employment and satisfying civic involvement possible. It helps to reiterate that the gap in the poverty rate between households headed by females and those by males is markedly greater for the official poverty rate than for the SPM. Unlike the official poverty rate, the SPM accounts for in-kind support, such as EITC and SNAP, that benefits female-headed households more than combined or male-headed households. These and other in-kind supports can significantly bolster women's basic capabilities, including the capability for median income.

Capability for fair opportunity requires more income for female-headed households, but it also requires support for employment and for civic activities for parents in all households with children. In addition to EITC, SNAP, WIC, and other current in-kind allowances, women could benefit more from refundable tax credits for children, paid parental leave by employers, subsidies for childcare, and publicly funded preschool education. These benefits can increase choices for women—but not only for women—regarding employment, family care, and civic participation. These choices are currently restricted because policies reinforce cultural and subcultural expectations that impinge more on women with children than on men. The structural changes recommended here would expand choices of outcomes for women without necessarily expecting equal outcomes for males and females in median or average income. In some cases, these supports will allow women to participate in lower-wage employment or civic affairs that do not earn income. It may be that some women will still prefer to devote more time and attention to birthing and rearing children. If they have the basic capability to make those choices, they should be able to choose. It is not always clear whether these "choices" are based in authentic gender differences or in the imposition of subcultural expectations by structural policies.

Data demonstrating disproportions in median income and education at levels beyond high school for some identifiable groups indicate unfair and unjust opportunities that exploit multiple individuals in those groups. Many individuals in these groups do not have the freedom fostered by basic capability that enables them to choose more income, education, and other outcomes—for example, civic involvement or time devoted to parenting—beyond the minimum. Furthermore, relevant quantitative and qualitative evidence helps us understand how structural changes to equalize—or nearly equalize, in the case of disabled persons—choices about more income, education, health, parenting time, civic involvement, and more are possible by expanding capabilities. In addition to disproportionate capabilities by race, disabilities, and gender, some basic capabilities are also denied lower SES persons of any race, gender, or disability status. These persons too will benefit from many of these structural adjustments.

Note that remedies for these inequalities transcend simple minimum capabilities such as minimum income or education. They include inequalities in fostering capabilities for higher outcomes in some areas. Think of efforts to alter recruitment practices and qualifications for employment and higher education when African Americans and lower SES persons with minimum basic capabilities have previously been denied opportunities to seek higher outcomes. Think of how the lack of maternity leave and provision for early childcare denies women and children opportunities to choose and achieve higher levels of income and more education.

Disproportionate opportunities at all levels of outcome require special attention to augment capabilities for those groups—for example, incarceration for young Black males and, to a lesser extent, for young White males. (The latter may help explain the decline in men relative to women who attend and graduate from college.) We should focus on fostering distinctive capability for disabled persons and address the distinctive cultural, subcultural, and biological and authentic gender identity circumstances of women with children. These group inequalities often require both quantitative and qualitative data. For example, the income and employment gap for women is statistically verifiable, but the injustice also requires qualitative information. How do we distinguish the plausible gender identity differences concerning child-rearing preferences from the effects of maternity policies, child tax credits, childcare subsidies, and early childhood education that reduce capability for employment and higher income? Statistics alone do not answer this question. We must observe and understand how these policies can expand and limit capabilities for choice. A significant portion of women may prefer a higher priority for child-rearing to maximizing employment outcomes. Some women (and a few men) also choose leadership in civic organizations rather than employment for higher income. Prohibiting prejudicial discrimination regarding qualifications is insufficient; structural changes must also foster basic capabilities. In some cases, the current structure almost forces choices that women and others would not make under fairer policies.

Minimal Basic Capabilities Not Sufficient

Attention to structural causes of disproportionate deficits in minimum basic capabilities for some groups is necessary but not sufficient to address all discrepancies in group income and advanced education levels. Nor does it adequately explain disproportions in group health and longevity or participation in community affairs and politics. Both qualitative and quantitative evidence reveal that Blacks and Latinx, disabled persons, women, and lower income persons—even those granted minimal basic capabilities—do not achieve the levels of income or education we would expect if they were truly free to express their preferences. These disproportionate outcomes are not likely due to irresponsible behavior. Higher level capacities are rarely distributed disproportionally by class, race and ethnicity, gender, and disabilities. Something is awry. Let's explore the data and qualitative observations regarding possible differences in higher level capabilities as distinct from capacities or irresponsible conduct.

INCOME GAPS

First, note that the gaps among White, Black, and Hispanic income exist in nearly equal portions at different income levels. To illustrate, a Pew Research Center study shows that in 2016, the gap between Black and Hispanic income at the 90th percentile and White income at the 90th percentile approximates the same percentage gap that occurs among the groups at median income for each group. Whites in the 90th percentile of income for their group received $117,986, while Blacks at the same percentile received $80,502 (68 percent of White income at the 90th percentile) and Hispanics received $76,847 (65 percent of White income at the 90th percentile). While we cannot easily specify the reasons for these racial gaps at higher income levels, we can be confident that neither individual choices about income outcomes nor any other explanations endemic to race or ethnicity account for the gaps.[41] There is no reason endemic to persons from these different racial groups as to why they would choose such significantly different income outcomes.

I reiterate that multiple individuals in each of these groups may not choose to pursue a higher income simply because of other more desirable outcomes—for example, a less lucrative but more satisfying line of employment or more leisure or family time is preferred. Equality of opportunity cannot be measured by income or any other singular outcome; however, a roughly equal proportion of equally capable segments of racial groups will likely choose higher incomes as a desirable outcome. Nothing endemic to being Black or Hispanic leads to preferring other outcomes to income, and nothing endemic to being White leads to preferring income over other competing outcomes. We can assume that a roughly equal proportion of Whites compared to other racial groups will prefer leisure, more family time, or satisfying but less-lucrative employment to maximum income. We can assume an equal proportion of Whites, Blacks, and Hispanics would, opportunities for choice being equal, choose to curtail income at an advanced level for the sake of other outcomes.

We should consider whether reduced opportunity explains these income gaps among the races at the higher income levels much as it does at the median income level. At these high levels of income, factors other than the absence of minimum basic capability are an even more likely part of the explanation. In the case of Asians and Latinx, unfair opportunity may not always or singularly be at play. The type of persons who immigrate and the reasons for which they immigrate may explain why Asians often receive a higher income than other racial groups (including Whites) and lower income than Whites at the highest 10th percentile of income for each group.[42] Many Latinx immigrating to escape poverty may also explain some of the income gap for them at different levels of income. Greater income mobility from first-generation to second-generation Latinx compared to White intergenerational mobility indicates that immigrant poverty and low income are temporary. It does not persist through generations. As noted earlier, empirical data demonstrate that Latinx immigrants often choose and achieve greater income in the second and third generations, indicating that these later generations are granted greater capability to achieve income outcomes. This characteristic of Latinx immigrants strongly suggests that some of the initial income gap is not entirely attributable to unfair, or at least long-term unjust, opportunities.[43]

For Blacks and (with some qualifications) many Hispanics, especially Latinx, qualitative evidence for unequal opportunity[44] explains some of these quantitative income gaps. The evidence points beyond unjust discrimination or even lack of minimum basic capability regarding qualifications for positions. The immediate cause of some of the income gap at higher levels can be explained by SES factors rather than race or ethnicity. To the extent that lower SES leads to unjust and unequal capabilities, it may explain unequal opportunity more directly than race. That is because a higher percentage of Blacks and Latinx than Whites are at a lower SES for historical reasons. Although the historical reasons for this SES inequality are racial and ethnic discrimination, one immediate cause is class, that is, economic and social deprivation.

These observations do not explain away current racial unfairness resulting from structural racism, but we need empirical analyses to discern where some of the causes are due to greater SES inequalities within different racial groups and which causes are principally racial. There is some of both, but I have consistently maintained that understanding and eradicating these injustices will require empirical analyses, not merely theories.

To extent that these SES factors are the most immediate cause of disproportionate income and education gaps for racial and ethnic groups, society can effectively foster equal capability by addressing the SES issues—for example, tax policy relative to income and wealth or Pell Grants for education. These encumbrances to income mobility limit capability and mobility for disproportionate numbers of Black or Latinx persons. The inequalities in mobility are not due directly to race, although they manifest themselves as disproportional outcomes among racial groups. Nor are they explained by lack of minimum income or a high school education. The effects of these impediments to equal opportunity exist for lower SES Whites too, but a higher percentage of Blacks and Latinx suffer from the failures to foster equal capabilities among SES classes. After all, these persons, as well as members of different racial and ethnic groups, begin with a disproportionately lower SES.

Just like Whites mired in disadvantages associated with class (not race or ethnicity), these disadvantages associated with class are more pronounced in some racial and ethnic groups. Put simply, there are more lower SES Blacks and Hispanics than Whites suffering from class disadvantages. Hence class disadvantage, as much as or more than race, explains part of the lack of real opportunities for Blacks and Latinx. Class disadvantages rob a higher portion of these racial groups of the capability to choose and execute outcomes associated with more income. In these cases, the problem is not primarily racial prejudice, either interpersonal or structural, but a higher proportion of class disadvantage.[45]

In addition to race gaps, data clearly show that socioeconomic mobility for all races in the United States is low. Nothing endemic to any group from the bottom 20 to 50 percent of the income range adequately explains why they remain disproportionately in the lower percentage brackets throughout their lives; the capability gap is explained by class. (See, for example, note 42 regarding inequality among Asians of different classes.) This lack of class mobility is partially explained by lack of minimum capability, but lower income groups above the lowest 20th percentile may also be burdened by an increasing inequality of income resulting from tax laws and institutional practices—for example, monopsony labor markets or neighborhood zoning—that widen the income gap for all persons and racial groups. A plethora of quantitative evidence from Raj Chetty at Harvard and others demonstrates that both intergenerational (i.e., from parents to their children) and intragenerational (i.e., throughout a person's life) mobility among multiple income percentiles in the United States is lower than in other nations and is becoming still lower.[46] The good news is that SES-focused initiatives to reduce this income gap are likely to increase disproportionately opportunities for Blacks, Latinx, and Native Americans. Since the racial and ethnic groups have disproportionally lower SES, they will disproportionally benefit from these race-neutral policies to improve income and educational mobility.

However, the income gap among the races at higher levels cannot be explained entirely by the class income gap. It is also race specific and traceable to historic and continuing institutions and practices that created and now perpetuate the income gap among these racial groups. Part of this perpetuation is inertia: the failure to take initiatives to change the patterns of hiring, continuing education, and promotion. This reality is sometimes labeled implicit (rather than intentional) racism.

Remedies

Changing these practices requires affirmation action. This affirmative action means changing practices that militate against promoting qualified minorities. (N.B.: Affirmative action, thus understood, should not be confused with race quotas or reverse discrimination, as it often is.) Affirmative action is not necessarily a practice to favor some racial minorities simply to meet a quota or a diversity goal. It can also seek to remove race-associated impediments to recognizing valid qualifications.

This kind of affirmative action does not push less-qualified persons up the employment or educational ladder. It changes established criteria for recruiting for hiring or for admission to educational institutions. Changing these patterns for recruitment and more careful attention to what constitutes genuine qualifications does not diminish the importance of qualifications or merit. It merely demands more attention to attracting qualified applicants from some racial and SES groups and to valid criteria for what we deem as qualified. What qualifies applicants also depends on what performance we expect from those who have received admission. If we expect only a high GPA, we need qualifications that predict the future GPA, but if we expect leadership and contributions to the community, we need to establish qualifications that accurately predict these results. Hence, affirmative action, well done, sharpens attention to genuine merit and qualifications rather than de-emphasizing them. It also questions tradition criteria of acceptance based solely on future GPAs.

Unfortunately, the latest US Supreme Court ruling against affirmative action at Harvard University and the University of North Carolina was based on the evolving practice since *Regents of the University of California v. Bakke* in 1978 of favoring racial groups based on the benefits of diversity that can override presumed "objective" criteria for admissions. Although I believe a temporary case for considering racial diversity might be justified for the same reasons that educational institutions and employers consider the benefits that diversity contributes to all at an institution in their admissions and hiring practices, the affirmative action I am endorsing here relies on other criteria. I note three of them: (1) recruitment of groups that have been unfairly overlooked in past recruitment; (2) considering disadvantages associated with adversity due to an individual's race; and (3) altering questionable criteria for admission and employment, such as favoring applicants whose family has attended a college or the prejudicial qualifications based on standardized tests and grades from high school. The good news is that Justice Roberts and cohorts both in concurrence and dissent in the Harvard and University of North Carolina cases granted latitude for these kinds of affirmative actions. Note that the affirmative action I advocate seeks to compensate for past unfair discrimination shrouded in the guise of "objective" criteria rather than to base admissions—or hiring, in the case of employers—on quotas for each racial group.[47] I will elaborate below.

As we have seen in other contexts, multiple other factors also under-cut normal opportunities for these racial groups—for example, lending practices that have traditionally failed to identify and accommodate Blacks, Latinx, or Native Americans. These practices include failure to publicize open positions at higher levels in business and the profes-sions in locations and in a manner that are likely to elicit applications from these minorities. Colleges and universities often recruit from a familiar pool of potential applicants and neglect other equally talented pools of prospects. In these cases too, various forms of affirmative action can mitigate the lack of capability of persons from some groups to present their qualifications for positions that offer higher levels of income. These compensatory actions to ensure fairness in consider-ing qualifications are themselves a form of reparation for past racial injustices, but they sharpen rather than compromise qualifications for appointments or admissions. Critics too often mistake this affirmative action for subverting qualifications. Sometimes what we have called qualifications unfairly favor faux qualities with which employers and admissions officers are accustomed. An applicant whose résumé makes us feel comfortable is not usually the most qualified. When we hear someone say, "That person looks like a Princeton student" or "That person will get along with his colleagues at his level," we should be suspicious. Qualifications should match long-term performance, not traditional criteria.

These forms of affirmative action are a type of reparations in that they expand opportunities for groups traditionally neglected because of unfair standards of qualification, but they are not direct redistributions of income. Some of them can also foster class opportunity and mobil-ity for all racial groups, for example, considering White applicants from geographical areas previously neglected. These efforts include racial and class integration of neighborhoods and school systems that promote security, networking, and educational advantages. They offer "real opportunity" for the current generation. Ill-considered income reparations may even be less effective in expanding capability for real opportunity. The reparations I am advocating are necessary to achieve fair equality of opportunity.

WEALTH GAPS: RACE AND CLASS

Unjust disparities in wealth among the races are even more pronounced than income inequality by race. According to the Board of Governors of the Federal Reserve, White families in 2019 held eight times as much net worth as Black families and five times as much as a typical Hispanic family.[48] These proportions were approximately the same for both median and mean net worth. The race disparities in wealth have profound consequences for fair opportunity.

As with minimum income and education, the wealth differentials are not limited to racial groups. A report from the Congressional Budget Office in 2019 shows that the wealth gap has grown for all citizens in the three decades since 1989. In 2019, the wealth held by the top 10 percent of families was 72 percent of all family wealth, compared to 63 percent in 1989. The percentage of wealth held by the top 1 percent increased from 27 percent to 34 percent over the same period. The percentage of wealth held by the entire bottom half declined from 4 to 2 percent.[49] Blacks and Hispanics have actually increased, although only marginally, in their percentages of wealth holdings.

The wealthiest families, of all racial groups, have increased their economic assets at a more rapid pace than the less wealthy. Some reports insist that increases in social security payments mitigate the wealth disparity. That may be true at lower levels of wealth disparity, but the consequences of disparity at higher levels measured in terms of influence in the political process and communities are not mitigated by social security income.

We should expect that some households choose to expand wealth and others do not. Many persons and households may prefer a less financially driven life and lack an interest in accumulating wealth, at least substantial wealth. Some prefer to accumulate wealth for inheritances and large charitable donations when they are elderly; others choose to consume or not to pursue wealth as a goal. But neither race nor class inequality of wealth can be fully explained by individual choices about desirable outcomes for well-being. As racial and class wealth inequality expand, the consequences for disparate influence in the political, civic, and cultural spheres become a threat to fair equality of opportunity. They leave less-wealthy persons, whether they belong to a racial or class group (or both), with reduced capability for influence and political clout. Fortunately, many policies, although not all, to correct this form of inequality address racial as well as class differences in opportunity. Most policies that reduce the wealth gap will expand fair opportunity for racial groups, as well as for lower SES persons in general. (As we have seen, Black, Hispanic, and Native Americans experience class inequality at higher rates than Whites, so reductions in class inequality of wealth will impact these groups more than Whites as a group.)

In some cases, wealth inequality by race has severe consequences for other forms of racial inequality—for example, funding to lobby against unjust incarceration and for or against unjust policing that impacts Blacks disproportionately (not exclusively). Some of these deleterious consequences for equal opportunity due to the wealth gap affect racial minorities more dramatically, whether or not the initial inequality arises due to race or class. If Black persons as a group are less able to lobby for policing or incarceration justice, it makes no difference whether their relative lack of wealth is due to class or racial causes.

Remedies

Multiple policy changes should be considered to reduce unequal capability to choose more or less wealth accumulation. The most consequential possibilities include the following.

1. Reducing the tax advantages for home ownership, especially the deduction for mortgage interest and local real estate taxes. Inequality in housing equity explains a significant portion of the wealth disparity at modest levels. These tax inequities solidify the inequality in ownership created by long-term racial discrimination in housing and lending for home mortgages. Eliminating or greatly reducing the tax deduction for mortgage interest and

instead offering a subsidy for first-time home buyers and borrowing for first-time homeownership would equalize the capability to choose homeownership. It would benefit Blacks and to some extent Latinx more than Whites. In some cases, affirmative action based on both race and class might be justified in housing and borrowing subsidies that would compensate for previous unjust practices. The focus should not be on redistributing income and wealth but on capability augmented by housing in safe neighborhoods.

2. Subsidies for loans to start small businesses—perhaps with some race-based affirmative action—could also allow for greater capability to choose a path toward wealth accumulation as well as options to earn an adequate income. Here again, the purpose of the subsidy should be to expand the capability for choices about desirable outcomes rather than to encourage specific outcomes or economic investments. There may be justifications for promoting small business or particular kinds of small business—for example, neighborhood restaurants based on the common good—but these affirmative action practices should be designed to increase capability for all disadvantaged groups to enhance their income and wealth along with community participation.

3. Current pension plans offering tax exemptions and deferred compensation often disproportionately benefit high-income employees to gain much higher pensions subsidized by tax benefits. For example, when an employer offers a tax exemption or a matching grant for a pension for an employee earning more than one hundred thousand dollars annually, the employee can afford the pension investment that a median income employee cannot. The higher earning employee benefits more from the exemption of taxes or matching pension grant than more modest income employees. Employees with lower incomes lose equal capability to make choices about savings. High-income earners are able to accumulate much more wealth for their retirement. Increasing standard set pensions, not as percentage of earnings, for all employees that include generous tax exemptions for these standard pension set-asides would offset the advantages higher income employees currently receive from employers matching pensions. Sometimes that tax-free pension set-aside for high-income employees doesn't even require a match. It is

targeted only to higher income employees. These pension plans offer much higher tax exemptions to higher income employees and exacerbate wealth disparities.

4. Taxing capital gains and dividends at a lower rate than other income allows investors with accumulated resources to obtain tax reductions unavailable to those with fewer resources. Lower capital gains rates should at least be limited to modest amounts of investments. Payment of "carried interest" to equity fund managers should be taxed at the regular rate, not at the lower capital gains rate. The carried-interest payment is for performance and not for investments, even if it is a proportion of the return received by the investor. Current reduced rates on capital gains on investments and on carried interest are purportedly justified on the grounds that they encourage greater investment in the economy. They may be good for society to some extent, but these tax benefits also offer increased after-tax income to already well-off persons. The income is based on already available wealth for investment rather than on active contributions to the economy. Allowance for lower capital gains tax targeting smaller investments would continue to encourage investment without benefiting the wealthiest investors.

5. Those with few resources for higher education incur educational debts and interest payments the well-off do not confront. Unless more government and private funds are offered to educate those who cannot pay outright for advanced education, the enormous debts and interest diminish the capability of many to bolster their desired education outcomes. Long-term income and wealth inequality follow. Expanding the Pell Grant program would clearly help diminish the wealth gap, and institutions should expand need-based financial support, as distinct from merit-based grants,[50] for their students.

6. I conclude these examples with the obvious benefits the nearly unlimited allowance for bequeathing and inheriting wealth provides for already wealthy families and their heirs. The policy of revising the cost-basis of equities and properties to the level at the time of the death of the person bequeathing exacerbates the problem of unlimited inheritance. This policy excuses both those bequeathing and those inheriting wealth from normal taxes on appreciation of the properties from the time of purchase to the

time of death of those bequeathing the wealth. Some persons and families will understandably seek to provide support for their heirs (often children); nevertheless, restricting the appreciation of wealth accumulation and the amount of inheritance that may be passed on to heirs does not undermine a reasonable opportunity for choice regarding saving and bequeathing wealth. Some saving for philanthropy is laudable, but excessive tax breaks for philanthropic investments gives greater choice for these investments to those with wealth. Choice for saving, bequeathing, and philanthropic investments can be encouraged without contributing dramatically to the increasing wealth gap. Here again, the current policy solidifies a long history of class and race disparity in wealth.

These and other current, largely race-neutral policies impact disparately on all persons with limited wealth. These policies may reduce or augment opportunities for choices about pensions, savings, and wealth for all persons. They impact Blacks, Latinx, and Native Americans with greater consequence because their wealth deficits are larger than most Whites and many Asians. In this instance, largely race-neutral policies—with some provisions for race-based affirmative action in housing, loan, and small-business subsidies—could remedy current limits on capability for making choices about outcomes for wealth. These remedies can be effective, even though the initial wealth gap between Blacks and Whites resulted from racist laws and not race-neutral policies. These remedies should be sufficient to address the race wealth gap as well as the widening class wealth gap.

EDUCATION GAPS FOR HIGHER LEVEL DEGREES

Educational achievements at a higher level are also disproportionate among the races, and again characteristics endemic to race cannot account for this inequality. Statista reports that in 2018, 35.2 percent of Whites, 25.2 percent of Blacks, 18.3 percent of Hispanics, and 56.5 percent of Asians held a college degree or more. Data from the American Council on Education from 2017 reinforce these findings. They also show that between 1997 and 2017, there were similar increases in the percentage of Whites and Blacks who received degrees. There was a slightly higher percentage increase in the overall percentage of Blacks receiving degrees. (Blacks with a college degree were increasing more rapidly as a percentage of the total number of Blacks.) The same report demonstrates that the racial discrepancies in degrees also include master's degrees, professional degrees, and PhDs. These data are largely confirmed by a 2021 Census Bureau report that concludes with the 2015–2019 period.[51]

Here again, Asians are more likely and Hispanics less likely to attain higher degrees, but they differ in group composition because of the high number of immigrants and their mixture of disparate motivations for immigrating. The differing levels of educational attainment for these groups may be attributable to these differing reasons for immigration rather than to unequal group capabilities our society provides for these racial and ethnic groups. Latinx persons are less likely to receive higher degrees than many East Asian persons, not because of favoritism toward Asians but as a factor of the percentage of first-generation immigrants and their reasons for immigrating. The proportion of Asians and Hispanics who complete degrees is a factor of who among them immigrates and the timing of their immigration, and not necessarily long-lasting impediments to individuals' choices. (We should note again that not all Asians or all Latinx should be lumped together. They arrive from significantly different nations and cultural backgrounds and should not be considered monolithically as Asian or Hispanic.)

Remedies

Despite these qualifications on how to interpret the data, we should look to factors other than individual choice about the desirability of more education for the differences in White, Black, and much of Hispanic education levels beyond high school. Fair equality of opportunity allows for equally capable persons to choose not to pursue higher levels of education and pursue other, for them, more desirable outcomes. This choice explains why some Blacks and Latinx will not choose four-year college and advanced degrees, but it does not account for why high proportions of Blacks or Latinx make that choice.

Some restrictions on the opportunity to choose advanced educational outcomes may be explained by disproportionate lack of basic capability due to low income and lack of a high school education for Blacks and Latinx. To the extent this explanation is accurate, a focus on previously discussed initiatives regarding minimal basic capability will advance opportunities for these groups. However, even casual observations indicate a need for other structural reforms to equalize opportunities for Blacks, many Hispanics, and for Native Americans. The racial and ethnic unfairness is not limited to lack of minimal capabilities. It includes unequal capabilities for choice among those who possess the minimal capabilities. These reforms will likely also be needed for working-class Whites, especially those from remote geographic areas.

We need affirmative action as special efforts to publicize opportunities for audiences heretofore marginalized in higher education and to offer special preparatory support to augment qualifications of promising applicants. These efforts should not be confused with unwarranted adjustments for less well-qualified applicants or to meet quotas. These special efforts should be designed to equalize capability for choosing advanced education. These affirmative actions can target potential applicants marginalized by class as well as by race. As noted above, they will include scrutiny of the precise criteria that qualify persons for admission. Some current criteria for qualification continue to favor characteristics more common among Whites and among men and women from well-off backgrounds and irrelevant to long-term performance.[52] Sometimes changes in the educational environment may be required to adjust for different backgrounds. These adjustments are analogous to altering circumstances to accommodate disabilities that have nothing to do with qualifications for academic or leadership performance over the long haul.

The Posse Foundation offers a vivid example of this kind of affirmative action. It selects students from disadvantaged backgrounds—often but not always from racial minority groups in urban areas—but with criteria more likely to measure their true qualifications for long-term and comprehensive (not merely academic in the classroom) performance. It also arranges for the receiving schools to adjust to these students from a different background and for the Posse students to adjust to quite foreign—not necessarily alien—environments. Posse's success in judging qualifications is demonstrated by a record that shows that its students achieve a GPA equal to other admitted students at particular schools, graduate at a higher rate than the typical student at the school they attend, and fill leadership roles in greater numbers. Put more succinctly, they achieve an equal GPA, better retention rates, and more measurable leadership activities than their peers at a school.[53]

Uncomfortable social settings due to ethnic differences or class differences may also require working with the more traditional students to help them become more welcoming to those from different cultural backgrounds. These are ways to bolster capability, and they accentuate and broaden rather than undermine educational opportunity based on merit.

In addition, educational institutions—sometimes with public support from governments or nonprofits—can expand the capability to choose advanced education with grants for persons with limited income and wealth. The high cost of advanced professional and graduate education can be prohibitive for qualified lower-middle-class applicants. These grants are not for the income-poor only. When limited financial resources discourage further educational attainment, merit and potential performance are downgraded and capability for choice is limited.

These structural reforms, which also require interpersonal adjustments by faculty and peer students, are and will continue to be necessary for fair equality of opportunity in education. Diversity of class and culture may be desirable for other reasons—for example, enriching the learning experience of all students and serving additional groups of people. Higher education benefits from students in the performing arts and athletics, considerations based on bringing diversity to the schools. The changes proposed here are, however, necessary for fair equality of opportunity alone. They are about fostering and recognizing qualifications for performance. They are not principally to advance the other benefits to the common good. As with the understanding of equal opportunity throughout this book, the adjustments recommended here supplement and do not undermine merit. They make it possible for persons who have not had a fair opportunity to demonstrate the required merit.

HEALTH AND LIFE-EXPECTANCY GAPS

Disproportionate group outcomes at levels beyond provision for minimum basic capability also occur in health and longevity. In this sphere, like others, some individuals will make choices that diminish their health or life expectancy. Some persons choose outcomes other than maximum health and the longest possible life. Others behave irresponsibly in nurturing their health preferences. That granted, individual choice, irresponsible behavior, and unalterable fate do not adequately explain the disproportionate poor health among some racial and ethnic groups and some geographical and economic groups. Unalterable fate refers to unexpected health events that cannot be changed by improving the capability to choose good health by public health and targeted interventions. Some, not all, of these group discrepancies in the quality of health and longevity of life can be explained by differences in provision for minimum income, education, and healthcare. What other factors cause group differences in health?

No one has written more exactingly and comprehensively about the trends and distribution of mortality and overall health among groups than Anne Case and Angus Deaton.[54] The age of mortality for middle-aged (forty-five to fifty-four) Whites without a bachelor's degree (BA) actually became younger between 1992 and 2017, with the principal causes of this decline in longevity being drug overdoses, alcoholism, and suicide—thus the title "deaths of despair." Although Black Americans die at even younger ages than Whites, the gap between them has diminished due to increasingly early mortality among Whites without a BA since the early 1990s. Blacks without a BA also die much earlier on average than those with a BA, and in the last decade Blacks without a BA have suffered a similar diminishment in longevity as Whites without a BA. The data seems incontrovertible that Blacks and Whites lacking a BA are much more prone to early deaths, often deaths by drug overdoses, alcoholism, and suicide.

Case and Deaton also consider poor health, especially pain, and its association with these maladies of despair. They believe self-reporting regarding pain is accurate because pain, broadly defined to include both perceived physical and mental hurting, is what persons feel. Pain, thus understood and reported, has increased dramatically among persons in their forties and fifties. There is no parallel in other developed countries, where reports of pain increase as persons age beyond sixty, not in midlife, as Case and Deaton are measuring in the United States. The increase in midlife pain in recent years occurs among those who lack a BA. The increased pain is not different for Blacks and Whites.

The increased pain correlates more with education than with race, even though a racial gap persists.

While it is not always clear what causes good and poor health or longer and shorter lives, we know that identifiable groups (e.g., racial, socioeconomic, and geographical) manifest disproportionate differences that cannot be explained merely by lack of minimum basic capability for health, by choice of outcomes, or by irresponsible behavior. Case and Deaton demonstrate that these early deaths and the associated poor health correlate with education short of a bachelor's degree, but they do not claim that the lack of higher education itself is the cause of the despair and early deaths. The increased pain and early death may be attributed more to societal attitudes toward and structural support for the working class, especially those in some geographical areas, than to a lack of education beyond high school. Deaton and Case also observe that chronic pain comes not so much from physically demanding work as from social exclusion of the working class.[55] Although the lack of a bachelor's degree correlates with both pain and deaths of despair, the underlying causes of the pain and deaths are not lack of a degree as much as changing socioeconomic conditions for the working class. These causes are manifested in expensive and inaccessible healthcare and the lack of uplifting work that bolsters self-esteem and respect. As Case and Deaton put it, the world in which less-educated American workers live is much more hostile than it was fifty years ago.[56]

Higher-level education and more income may be factors in fostering the greater capability for the working class of all races and ethnic groups, but other initiatives are likely more important. They free persons to choose outcomes other than higher education or income. Hence, persons could choose not to pursue advanced education or greater income without sacrificing their opportunity for good health.

Case and Deaton focus most on the high cost and inaccessibility of healthcare for the working class. These factors are driven by pharmaceutical companies and healthcare providers, some of whom have pushed opioids for profits more than for health, and by the failure to provide effective public health and healthcare for diseases associated with pain and despair. The lack of work offering the social basis of self-respect, exacerbated by atrophied labor unions and cultural attitudes disparaging some forms of work, also contribute to this group malaise. "Rent-seeking" monopolies and monopsonies seeking inordinate profits, salaries, and returns on investment for powerful and unregulated employers also contribute to income inequality. Perhaps more damaging, these cultural and economic attitudes lead to a loss of the social basis of self-respect of the high school–educated working class.[57]

We should conclude that fostering the capability to choose better health and long lives requires more than minimum education and income—and even more than basic healthcare. Pursuing education beyond high school is not necessary to expand the capability for choosing better health. That capability requires an economic structure and a culture that affirm the value of working-class life.

Remedies

Policies and practices to augment these aspects of capability will include, most of all, control of the cost of pharmaceutical and other medical technology where hospitals and the most profitable physicians are often able to seek "rent" beyond the innovations needed for effective competition. Case and Deaton repeatedly cite Kenneth Arrow's well-established work insisting that just healthcare is not possible through the free market. The problem is not free markets per se but that medical markets cannot be free and just because of the inequalities of information and thus control of these markets for selfish purposes. Case and Deaton call for more attention to public health issues—especially mental health—among the working class and those associated with incarceration. Lack of attention to mental health care is also associated with addictions of various kinds.[58] Finally, Deaton and Case contend that we need to do more to support unions—especially in manufacturing—and to avoid monopolistic and monopsonistic control of consumer and labor markets, for example, company towns, long after innovative entrepreneurs have been duly rewarded for their productive contributions. We should add that changing cultural and political attitudes and more information regarding these measures will help create a climate favorable for changes in policy and practices.[59] Maybe this book has something along these lines to contribute.

PARTICIPATION IN FAMILY, CIVIC,
AND POLITICAL AFFAIRS

Case and Deaton also note reduced participation in key institutions among Whites without a BA. Blacks were, for the most part, already limited in participation, but for both racial groups, lack of participation and decreasing participation in recent decades have been more prominent among persons with less than a BA. Case and Deaton focus on a variety of institutions. They include marriage and childbearing and consider religious communities a part of community and civic life. (We are interested in other civic organizations as well.) Case and Deaton use voting as a measure of political participation. These activities are choices followed by responsible behavior for their execution. Working-class persons—of all races—have not been choosing to participate in equal proportion to others in society. Since the diminution of participation among this group is recent—high school graduates from the working class formerly participated in higher proportions—the declining participation cannot be attributable to a lack of higher education alone. It is attributable to factors other than, or at least in addition to, more education among high school–educated working-class persons. Again, there is no obvious explanation for the disproportionate "choices" among this group, but society is in some way impeding participation. We are failing to foster the capability for working-class participation.

Once again, Case and Deaton do not insist that family, civic, and political participation equal well-being. These outcomes are appropriately left to choice—although collective moral encouragement could be beneficial—and specific outcomes are not a conclusive measure of well-being. However, Case and Deaton observe that greater participation is often self-reported as linked with satisfaction and better health. Evidence also shows that high levels of participation in marriage (or stable cohabitation) for childbearing is similarly associated with fostering capability and fair opportunity for children. Once again, Case and Deaton link the opportunity to choose and successfully achieve desirable outcomes with causes beyond more—or in addition to—income and education. Although levels of family and civic participation correlate with higher education and higher than median income, we should not confuse that correlation with causation. Other societal factors impinging on the working class and minority racial groups have diminished these persons' opportunities for participation. Prior to recent changes in culture and social structure, the White working class participated at a higher rate. Although Case and Deaton do not consider incarceration in this context, we know that excessive incarceration and failure to ameliorate its effects have impeded participation, especially for Black and working-class men. Recent political, cultural, and economic structures have discouraged participation for working-class Americans, and increasingly so for the White working class.[60]

Fair opportunity requires that we understand and abolish these impediments to working class participation. Case and Deaton repeatedly assert that the problem is not capitalism or all markets. It seems that the US cultural and political climate has increasingly discouraged working class participation in family, community, and political affairs.

Since working class participation among non–college graduates has been higher in the past, we cannot expect minimal basic capabilities alone to reverse this participation deficit among the working class. Aggressively promoting college education or active participation in these institutions could restrict freedom for pursuing desirable outcomes and further diminish societal respect for the high-school-graduate working class. Granting these observations, we need to consider special impediments for a higher percentage of Black, Hispanic, Native American, and White non-college-graduate working-class persons, particularly Black males, to participate in these ways.

Remedies

Changing those impediments without thwarting choice about marriage, child-rearing, and civil and political involvement will require many of the same policies and changes in the societal culture that Case and Deaton called for regarding free choice regarding health. These include low-cost and accessible healthcare and equal support for public health for all groups; employment that rewards persons fairly by diminishing monopsonistic control of labor markets; and prudent labor regulations and compensation—for example, minimum wages and ETIC—that correct labor markets' failure to reward the productivity of the working class. Reducing purposeless incarceration without evidence that it limits crime and supporting efforts to allow formerly incarcerated persons to choose greater civic and political participation will also expand capability for the working class of all races, especially Black males. These policies may include changes as simple as permitting formerly incarcerated persons to vote in elections.

These remedies call for greater palpable benefits for working-class high school graduates, but these benefits are ultimately more about social respect than merely about material well-being. Capability for participation requires societal respect for the working class, a standard increasingly ignored by the economic and political elites of varied political persuasions. These cultural changes require individual behavior that interacts with policy and political structures. The focus should not be exclusively on structural changes.

CONCLUDING REMARKS: WHAT FAIR EQUALITY OF OPPORTUNITY REQUIRES

Fair equality of opportunity requires much more than rewarding the most qualified while ignoring how persons become qualified. It requires the minimal capability to choose among desired outcomes and become qualified for executing those choices. It requires that we consider why some groups—for example, of different racial and ethnic backgrounds, sometimes women, disabled persons, and often the working class—are not proportionally represented in achieving outcomes beyond those for minimal capability.

Fair equality of opportunity understood in this way requires nurturing positive freedom and goes beyond negative rights that restrict intrusions by others. It includes positive rights that can be satisfied only by proactive behavior and policies, not simply by refraining from interference with individuals' lives. Equality of opportunity, as almost any moral principle, can be misused in efforts to justify behavior antithetical to a full and accurate understanding of what it requires. Among the most common misuses of this principle is the claim that it permits and requires the freedom to pursue any individual or group end other than denying other persons positions based on their qualifications. (During the civil rights debates in the sixties, even the freedom to conduct business in a prejudicial manner was declared by some to be a just opportunity preserved by the "free market." Lester Maddox's refusal to serve Black patrons in his restaurant was a vivid example. Merchants were thought to be justified in selling to whomever they chose, and employers were considered morally and legally free to hire whomever they wished.) We sometimes hear that equal opportunity permits persons to advance their power and greed in the "free market" without limitations to require that power and money foster the capabilities of others. I have tried to demonstrate that this criticism is valid in some instances and have explained in some detail why and how some individual freedoms must be curtailed to promote capability and fair opportunity for others.

We also hear, for example, that persons should be free to control their own bodies, which entails freedom from coercion to take or reject vaccines or to employ safety measures (e.g., wear seat belts in automobiles). Evidence conclusively demonstrates that such restrictive measures are sometimes morally and sometimes legally necessary to protect the capability (and freedom) of others to choose good health.

I have also rejected this absolute freedom regarding the right of pregnant women to have abortions. However, I reject legal coercion in that case because of the special burden on these women. They should have a right and the freedom to decide what moral values are at stake. They should not be above moral counsel and criticism, but they are acutely aware of the consequences of abortion or no abortion for themselves *and* for their close associates and family members. Pregnant women bear the burden of the consequences, not only for themselves but also for those around them, of their moral judgments regarding abortion. The state has no right to exercise coercion in these cases until the fetus is viable. On the other hand, I have maintained that pregnant women should be, if feasible, legally required not to harm a fetus by ingesting alcohol or drugs. This is not a casual affirmation of the moral freedom of pregnant women to do whatever they wish with their bodies.

Fair equality of opportunity requires that we, as a society, enact and forge structural changes that remove impediments to proportionate outcomes by different groups in various areas of education, income, wealth, good health and longevity, and participation in society's institutions. It also requires that we foster renewed capabilities for those who have lost the full capability to choose and execute desired outcomes, whether or not that loss is caused by fate, injustice, or irresponsible behavior. (This renewal still requires individuals and groups to take responsibility for their outcomes and to merit those outcomes once they have been granted equal capabilities. It does not demand identical or even equal outcomes for everyone.) It does require that we nurture capabilities as equally as possible throughout lifetimes, even as persons inevitably encounter disruptions and require capabilities appropriate to their age.

The obligation to foster capabilities is individual as well as structural. It requires stable and nurturing parenting of children. It requires affirming the dignity and right to fair opportunity among those we encountered as well as those with whom we have close relationships. It requires that we individually contribute to a culture that nurtures policies, practices, and structures that advance fair equality of opportunity. It also requires that individuals support just structures that foster, insofar as possible, equal capabilities for choosing and executing the outcomes we choose.

In so doing, fair equality of opportunity preserves the freedom of persons to choose and take responsibility for the outcomes they believe advance their well-being or goals in life. Recall again the example of Martin Luther King Jr. and also, more commonly, of military, police, firefighters, nonprofit workers, and others who believe their satisfaction and true well-being require what many of us consider unacceptable sacrifices.

These considerations require that we collectively rethink the cliché of equal opportunity that we have sometimes unthinkingly embraced. A careful rethinking of fair equality of opportunity demands a more comprehensive and specific examination of what agents and actions are needed for a better approximation of fair equality of opportunity. We now turn to that task.

NOTES

1. Much of my discussion of child development relies heavily on two publications of *From Neurons to Neighborhoods*. These documents demonstrate that science shows that development on which all children depend begins with conception, irrespective of one's views about the legal and moral permissibility of abortion. Pregnant women who do not anticipate an abortion are morally—and in extreme cases legally—responsible to foster the capability of the fetus. Their family and friends are also responsible to encourage and support the future mother's behavior nurturing this end.

Readers may also want to refer to a recent Consensus Study Report of the National Academy of Sciences, *A Roadmap to Reducing Child Poverty*, edited by Greg Duncan and Suzanne Le Menestrel (Washington, DC: The National Academy Press, 2019). This volume also informs my comments on capabilities for children, although it focuses more exclusively on income measurements of poverty and capability than I do.

2. The official poverty threshold adjusts for inflation but not for the changes in these essential expenses. Thus the SPM threshold is higher than the official poverty threshold. In 2020 the extra payments measured by the SPM for the first time exceeded the higher threshold for the SPM, which explains why the poverty rates are lower relative to the official rate.

3. The 2023 Census Bureau report on poverty appeared subsequent to my writing this chapter. I will not update all the data from the OFM and SPM, but I will note the significant increase in child poverty for the SPM from 2021 to 2022 as measured by the 2023 report. The SPM child poverty rate increased by 7.2 percent to 12.4 percent. The SPM child poverty rate remains below the OFM poverty rate due to in-kind assistance and tax credits being counted, but the child poverty rate for the SPM has more than doubled, primarily due to changes in the child tax credit. Policies make a difference in provision for minimal capability and "real opportunity," in this case for children! See www .census.gov/content/dam/Census/newsroom/press-kits/2023/iphi/20230912 -iphi-slides-poverty.pdf.

4. The data cited are taken from "Poverty in the United States: 2021" (US Census Bureau), www.census.gov/content/dam/Census/library/publications /2022/demo/p60-277.pdf, and an OECD report on poverty rates, https://data .oecd.org/inequality/poverty-rate.htm.

5. The SPM, due in large part to considering in-kind public grants for special needs (e.g., nutrition for children in the household) and tax refunds, has shown significant progress in reducing child poverty, even after considering the significant increase in child poverty in 2022. (See note 3.) The SPM also provides better information for how society supports disadvantaged demographic groups by looking at factors beyond cash income. The significance of in-kind assistance and tax advantages for low-income families along with essential expenditures that cannot be avoided further demonstrates the inadequacy of strictly cash income measurements for unequal and inadequate capability and opportunity. Unfortunately, the disproportionality of poverty among demographic groups remains for both the official and the supplemental measurements.

6. Relief through interpersonal and nonprofit charitable donations to low-income families, although useful, cannot alone remedy this failure to provide for minimal income on a generalized or universal scale.

7. See Statista's "Educational attainment distribution in the United States from 1960 to 2022," https://www.statista.com/statisticr/184260/educational -attainment-in-the-us/.

8. It may already be obvious that these minimal outcomes for basic capability are interactive and mutually reinforcing.

9. Anne Case and Angus Deaton, *Deaths of Despair and the Future of Capitalism* (Princeton, NJ: Princeton University Press, 2020).

10. I hasten to add, out of deference and respect for several non–high school graduates, that there are many without this minimal education who have been enabled to achieve in other outcomes, for example, income, health, and prestigious employment. These remarkable exceptions highlight the correlative and causal relationships.

11. Some critics of Head Start funding hold that evidence does not demonstrate that it increases test score performance for the long-term. Heckman and many others cite evidence that Head Start, even though the quality could be improved, has positive effects on long-term behavior: students remaining at class level and staying in school through a high school degree. Other more expensive early-childhood programs have even more profound long-term effects and are shown to be cost-effective in expanding capability for basic education as well as civic behavior. Some readers may want to view "Early Childhood Education" by Heckman et al. (2015) at https://heckmanequation .org/www/assets/2017/01/FINALMoffitt-ECE-Paper2015.pdf.

12. See *Whither Opportunity? Rising Inequality, Schools, and Children's Life Chances*, edited by Greg J. Duncan and Richard J. Murnane (Russell Sage Foundation, 2011) and *Restoring Opportunity: The Crisis of Inequality and the Challenge for American Education* by Greg J. Duncan and Richard J. Murnane (Harvard Education Press, 2014). Duncan and Murnane give less attention than I do to secondary school as a terminal degree adequate for many to choose outcomes they desire to pursue—and thus more attention to higher education for opportunity.

13. Some cosmetic and other satisfying enrichments can be left to individual choice; however, debilitating appearance and diminished physical potential can also prohibit choices about other outcomes. Access to dental care and eyecare must also be included to ensure good health to financially less well-off citizens, both the young and elderly.

14. See "US Health Care Coverage and Spending" (Congressional Research Services, 2021), https://sgp.fas.org/crs/misc/IF10830.pdf.

15. See Liana E. Fox and Kalee Burns, "The Supplemental Poverty Measure: 2020," www.census.gov/content/dam/Census/library/publications/2021/demo/p60-275.pdf.

16. See "Health Insurance Coverage of the Total Population," www.kff.org/other/state-indicator/total-population/?currentTimeframe=0&sortModel=%7B%22colId%22:%22Location%22,%22sort%22:%22asc%22%7D, and "Status of State Medicaid Expansion Decisions: Interactive Map," www.kff.org/

medicaid/issue-brief/status-of-state-medicaid-expansion-decisions-interactive
-map/.

17. See "Tracking Health Insurance Coverage in 2020–2021" (Office of Health Policy, October 29, 2021), https://aspe.hhs.gov/sites/default/files/documents/2fb03bb1527d26e3f270c65e2bfffc3a/tracking-insurance-coverage-2020-2021.pdf.

18. See "Health Insurance Coverage in the United States: 2020," www.census.gov/content/dam/Census/library/publications/2021/demo/p60-274.pdf.

19. See "Are Out-of-Pocket Medical Expenses Covered by ADA?" (Intuit TurboTax), https://turbotax.intuit.com/tax-tips/health-care/are-out-of-pocket-medical-expenses-covered-by-aca/L6SmjGAx4.

20. This statement allows for rational persons to view the conceptus having the same moral status of a human, but that is not a moral perspective that all rational persons have or that should be codified into law, which is universally restrictive.

21. They might still be legally liable for drug and alcohol consumption and other abusive behavior that jeopardizes the health of a potential human with no notable benefit to themselves.

22. See note 1 for full bibliographical data on this volume.

23. Some readers may wish to see Thomas Edsall's column in the *New York Times* citing scholarship addressing this role of parenting in fostering capability for young males, www.nytimes.com/2021/09/22/opinion/economy-education-women-men.html?smid=em-share.

24. See www.youtube.com/watch?v=ca_N4vWnVnM&list=PLXEYyGucb AbqsBuS2otsVLgnskC3yhOc7&index=1&t=21s for a moving presentation by Ms. Haggerty of the Community Solutions approach.

25. Recent hate crimes in the wake of the US response to COVID-19 may change this threat of violence against persons of Asian origin. Neighborhood violence differs from hateful acts by persons beyond neighborhoods.

26. We have ample evidence that some groups of people are almost coaxed into detrimental behavior by other interpersonal (e.g., family abuse) and structural (e.g., a phenomenally high rate of incarceration for African American males or readily available drugs for pain relief) conditions than by totally or even partially self-inflicted behavior. We justly praise those who resist these temptations and detriments to their freely chosen well-being, but we cannot expect seizing opportunities to be acts of heroism. In some cases, the criminal justice system mistreats the innocent or mildly detrimental behavior by racial groups or lower SES groups. A criminal justice system and incarceration are, of course, also necessary to judge, deter, and halt irresponsible behavior that threatens opportunities for others.

27. Readers may be interested in Bruce Western, *Punishment and Inequality in America* (New York: Russell Sage Foundation, 2006) and *Homeward: Life in the Year After Prison* (New York: Russell Sage Foundation, 2018).

28. I remind readers that the concepts of grace, merit, desert, and judgment informing the observation and claims in this paragraph are often used, implicitly or explicitly, by social scientists, philosophers, and others who have no interest in theological arguments. Their use of these concepts is nonetheless often richly informed by religious and theological thinking as well. There are ample possibilities for mutual dialogue among persons with these different perspectives or different comprehensive views. We should neither verify recommendations because they emanate from a religious tradition nor dismiss them for that reason. But we should not reject well-reasoned arguments merely because they emanate from a specific religious source or tradition. We should always consider the merits of the reasoning offered. This reasoning is not always bound to authoritarian documents or leaders. We should also note that persons who become disabled may be somewhat responsible for their disability. Accidents are rarely totally without some culpability of the injured.

29. These jarring data call for specific references to Bruce Western, *Punishment and Inequality in America*, 26–29.

30. See "If You Paid Your Debt to Society, You Should Be Allowed to Work" (*New York Times*, August 4, 2021), www.nytimes.com/2021/08/04/opinion/clean-slate-incarceration-work.html.

31. I have also noted an additional qualification regarding some disabled persons; the realities of some disabilities render it impossible for structural adjustments to equalize different capabilities. However, less than equal capability should not be confused with the inability to foster capabilities as they are feasible.

32. See "Annual median earnings for people with and without disabilities in the US from 2008 to 2021" (Statista), www.statista.com/statistics/978989/disability-annual-earnings-us/.

33. Some may wish to consult *Streets of Gold: America's Untold Story of Immigrant Success* by Ran Abramitzky and Leah Boustan (New York, Hachette Book Group, 2022) for a thorough and statistically informed account of immigrant opportunities and successes in the United States. It seems that although fair opportunity for immigrants has not been ideal, the second-generation immigrant population has been one area in which our society has more closely approximated the ideal than it does for other groups.

34. See "Educational Attainment in the United States: 2015" by Camille L. Ryan and Kurt Bauman, www.census.gov/content/dam/Census/library/publications/2016/demo/p20-578.pdf. The disproportion among some disabled persons may be explained by barriers to education that cannot be easily remediated by changing circumstances or therapeutic help. On the other hand, some

disabilities may make advanced education a more feasible aspiration than other outcomes for which capability is more diminished. Adequate measurement of unfair options for disabled persons will require fine-grained data about the nature of the disabilities and the best avenues for advancing equal or nearly equal capabilities for education outcomes.

35. This datum may seem peculiar because Asians are more likely than Whites to have received higher education degrees, but keep in mind that Asian immigrants are from different countries and Asian immigrants' education status varies markedly, some from highly educated backgrounds and others from poorly educated backgrounds, with fewer at the median levels.

36. See "Educational Attainment in the United States: 2015."

37. See "Poverty in the United States: 2021" " for these Census Bureau reports on poverty, and note that the data, especially for the supplemental measure, are skewed by COVID and COVID-related stimulus payments. Disabled persons receive more in-kind assistance, and only the SPM measures in-kind assistance as income; hence the differences in the OFM and the SPM poverty income for disabled persons.

38. As explained in note 3, the 2022 child poverty rate has become much higher due to policy changes following the initial respond to COVID-19.

39. See "Gender pay gap in U.S. hasn't changed much in two decades" (Pew Research Center, 2023), www.pewresearch.org/fact-tank/2021/05/25/gender -pay-gap-facts/.

40. None of these explanations for gender income inequality explain unequal pay for the same or similarly demanding work. That inequality is never justified and violates the lowest standard for equality of opportunity, *viz.*, prejudice base on gender alone.

41. While, as we anticipate, Asian income at the 90th percentile ($133,529) is even higher than White income at that level, income inequality is much more pronounced among Asians than among other groups. At the 10th percentile for their racial/ethnic group, Asians received only $12,478, markedly less than Whites at the 10th percentile ($15,094). As we shall observe in this chapter, class differences may in some cases better explain capability gaps than some race differences. Who immigrates to the United States at what time in their lives and from what Asian country may also be a factor shaping these data. See Pew Research Center's "Income Inequality in the U.S. Is Rising Most Rapidly Among Asians" (July 12, 2018), www.pewresearch.org/social-trends/2018/07 /12/income-inequality-in-the-u-s-is-rising-most-rapidly-among-asians/.

42. We must also keep in mind that Asians, and to some extent Latinx, emigrate from quite different countries and for different reasons. Persons from Vietnam and Cambodia in the middle 1970s immigrated for different reasons and varied sharply in their capabilities than immigrants from Japan and India. The point here is not the different preferences and qualifications of the various

ethnic groups. It is rather who decided to emigrate for what reasons from these different nations.

43. The distinction between unfair and unjust implies that there may be times when unfair arrangements exist as a matter of uncontrollable changes that are beyond most structural injustices in the United States. For example, forces in other societies driving immigration lead to the limited opportunity for these immigrants rather than structural injustices in the United States. This unfairness dissipates overtime as the unequal capabilities are diminished in a relatively just society. The significant mobility between first- and second-generation Latinx immigrants fits with this structural account of unfairness and justice. There is injustice, but it is not necessarily long lasting.

44. As I have suggested, this unequal and unfair opportunity in the first generation of Latinx immigrants fleeing poverty may not be grossly unjust. That is because we cannot expect that a receiving nation will immediately foster equal capabilities to immigrants fleeing poverty. The United States should, however, do more to foster multiple capabilities among Latinx immigrants.

45. Here again in this context, we must note that some of the differences are long-standing structural differences initially precipitated by racial prejudice, such as those emanating from zoning laws specifically designed to segregate races and relegate some races to dilapidated neighborhoods and vestiges of legal redlining that prohibited banks and real estate agents from loaning and promoting sales in minority neighborhoods.

46. See "Economic Mobility in the United States" from the Pew Charitable Trust and the Russell Sage Foundation at www.pewtrusts.org/~/media/assets /2015/07/fsm-irs-report_artfinal.pdf and Raj Chetty at Opportunity Insights, https://opportunityinsights.org. These data are sophisticated and useful, but they unfortunately measure mobility exclusively by income to the exclusion of other outcomes, such as participation in communities and families, that persons might choose.

47. Readers may wish to consult the Justices' opinions in *Students for Fair Admission, Inc. v. President and Fellows of Harvard College* and *Students of Fair Admission, Inc. v. University of North Carolina*, www.supremecourt.gov/ opinions/22pdf/20-1199_hgdj.pdf.

48. See "Disparities in Wealth by Race and Ethnicity in the 2019 Survey of Consumer Finances" (Federal Reserve System, September 28, 2020), www .federalreserve.gov/econres/notes/feds-notes/disparities-in-wealth-by-race-and -ethnicity-in-the-2019-survey-of-consumer-finances-20200928.html.

49. See "Trends in the Distribution of Family Wealth, 1989 to 2019" (Congressional Budget Office), https://www.cbo.gov/publication/58533.

50. Merit should be considered for admission, but merit-based grants often become a means for attracting students from wealthy families rather than a measure of qualifications required to perform adequately. This process

excludes students from families with even modest need from receiving equal consideration based on merit. Some might argue that generous grants based on need and modest government debt relief may subsidize higher education for the middle class, but the magnitude of debt incurred in obtaining higher education degrees can make individual choice for this education virtually infeasible. Modest education debt is commensurate with fair equality of opportunity. Those who choose higher education at all levels should expect to incur some debt commensurate with the financial returns they are likely to receive resulting from the degrees. Colleges and universities should also be expected to support a significant portion of need-based grants via taxes and wealthy donors.

51. See "Percentage of educational attainment in the United States in 2018, by ethnicity" (Statista), www.statista.com/statistics/184264/educational -attainment-by-enthnicity; https://1xfsu31b52d33idlp13twtos-wpengine.netdna -ssl.com/wp-content/uploads/2019/02/REHE-Chapter-1-SA.pdf; and "Bachelor's Degree Attainment in the United States: 2005 to 2019" (US Census Bureau), www.census.gov/content/dam/Census/library/publications/2021/acs/ acsbr-009.pdf.

52. Perhaps the most prominent example of misplaced criteria for admission occurs with heavy reliance on tests for qualification. Those who can afford tutoring for these tests gain an advantage that belies their qualifications or the quality of their eventual performance. We should also measure performance by contributions to the learning community, which does not mean contribution by mere diversity but also considers leadership, remaining in school, and new learning initiatives rather than narrow measures, such as class rank according to GPA.

53. Visit the Posse Foundation at www.possefoundation.org.

54. See Case and Deaton, *Deaths of Despair.*

55. Ibid., 92.

56. Ibid., 243.

57. Michael Sandel offers similar observations and conclusions in *The Tyranny of Merit.*

58. See "Experts Say We Have the Tools to Fight Addiction. So Why Are More Americans Overdosing Than Ever" by Jeneen Interlandi (*New York Times*, June 24, 2022), www.nytimes.com/2022/06/24/opinion/addiction -overdose-mental-health.html?searchResultPosition=1.

59. Readers may find Nicholas Kristof's August 2023 *New York Times* column on Oliver Anthony's "Rich Men North of Richmond" relevant to this cultural attitude. See www.nytimes.com/2023/08/30/opinion/oliver-anthony -liberals.html?searchResultPosition=10.

60. See chapter 12 of *Deaths of Despair* for the crux of this argument.

Chapter 4

Agents and Actions Required

I have contended that fair equality of opportunity involves both structural alterations and individual obligations to others. The structural considerations must be achieved by governments at all levels, as well as by institutions (including civic organizations and for-profit entities). These structural changes must be supported by citizens, including group action by those denied fair equality of opportunity. The individual actions can and must be wrought by family members, friends, associates in the workplace, and initiatives by fellow citizens. In sum, fair equality of opportunity, I am arguing, requires multiple actors and actions at many levels.

Note that much more is required than governments and institutions protecting individuals' freedom from unfair restrictions that inhibit their pursuit of well-being. Fair opportunity requires multiple actions to ensure persons and groups positive freedom via capabilities to choose and advance their well-being or goals. Moreover, fostering these capabilities occurs throughout lifetimes, not only at some starting line.

STRUCTURAL OBLIGATIONS

Governments

Government, at various levels, has multiple obligations to secure structural changes necessary for individuals and families to secure capability to choose and pursue well-being. As previously indicated, these structural changes require an array of policies pertaining to child development, criminal justice, disabilities, education, inequalities of income and wealth that impede opportunity, and protections for civic and political participation and organizing. I have explained why these policies must be adjusted over time to respond to disrupted opportunities caused by structural injustices (e.g., racist criminal justice policy or inadequate assurance of crucial healthcare and public health) and unanticipated events (e.g., injuries or sickness or revised goals). These adjustments include helping persons recover from irresponsible actions that continue to impede their choice and progress when they are ready to move forward (e.g., from incarcerations or failures to meet employment responsibilities).

They also require enabling persons denied opportunities to access government assistance that may have been cut off due to incarceration (e.g., as simple as access to public assistance or healthcare insurance). These persons also need possibilities (e.g., as simple as restoring voting privileges) to organize for political, social, and cultural change that foster basic and equal capability. Persons lacking full opportunity can still be agents for change. Indeed, their participating in the process of change is one means of expanding their opportunity. There are many instances of the positive effects that foster capability for persons who organize to overcome injustices to themselves. The political structure must enable political participation. In addition, structural adjustments (e.g., access to in-home healthcare or specialized institutional senior care) are necessary to foster capabilities related to aging as it inhibits mobility and memory. Once again, merely bringing persons to an equal starting point is not enough.

Action for these structural policies requires every level of government. State and local governments can be more flexible to accommodate more local needs for policies such as zoning laws, sales tax, and taxes needed to fund state and local community needs. They can also offer legislation and executive action when other states and the federal government are slow to act, such as enabling political participation by formerly incarcerated persons or support for early childhood day care and education. State and local government is necessary but never sufficient to address overall tax policy (e.g., regarding capital gains taxes, heritance taxes, mortgage interest deductions). Federal legislation and executive action are also necessary when some states fail to act regarding matters such as child income poverty, early childhood day care and education, necessary restrictions on child labor, zoning that leads to housing segregation of groups, public health (e.g., climate control), and support for public education at all levels. This need for federal action now also includes provision for women to make moral choices about their health, the needs of their families, and pregnancy. Minimum standards of justice are necessary for all citizens and residents of a nation. States' rights must not include failing to provide fair equality of opportunity for all—for example, a supposed right to make healthcare contingent on employment. In some instances, the federal government is obligated to foster fair opportunity when states fail to act. A common morality demands federal action, and congressional and executive action are possible even where constitutional rights do not obtain. For example, while no one would claim a constitutional right to paid parental leave or a refundable child tax credit, I have argued for national legislation to support both.

Nongovernmental Institutions

In addition to government action, structural justice requires voluntary support from nongovernmental institutions. These institutions—both private and civic, including colleges and universities—can adjust quickly to acute needs that call for emergency and experimental efforts (e.g., efforts to assuage hunger or education deficits unattended to by governments) and offer advocacy for new government policies. We have witnessed examples of these kinds of initiative in recent corporate responses to laws pertaining to reproductive health and non-heterosexual marriage. These organizations can also facilitate individual access to government programs such as childcare, Medicare and healthcare for all persons, and housing subsidies. In addition, labor organizations must enhance individual opportunities, and for-profit entities must be responsive to the needs of employees in ways compatible with, but that go beyond, their immediate economic self-interests. Labor organizations and for-profits must, for example, be sensitive to the needs of disabled persons and racial minorities as well as unexpected illnesses, parental care, and care for senior family members. Opportunities for these persons depend on changes in employment practices and work arrangements and schedules for which labor unions can bargain and which employers can adopt efficiently and voluntarily. They can include affirmative action (consistent with merit) to overcome deficits in opportunity for racial minorities and for those unfairly limited by their socioeconomic factors beyond their capabilities to adapt, for example, neighborhoods that fail to support education. Employers should also adjust policies to support family structures and practices—for example, paid maternity and paternity leave—that foster opportunities for vulnerable family members and that accommodate choices regarding marriage and gender affirmation, for example, legal recognition for gay and lesbian partners.

These voluntary efforts are never adequate without the more coercive policies of governments, but they are often more flexible than government in accommodating specific circumstances. They can rise to the occasion when governments are slow or awkward in responding to identifiable structural injustices. They can offer new initiatives, experiments that may illustrate what could be possible on a universal scale. The Perry School and the Abecedarian Early Intervention Project for early-childhood education are vivid examples.[1] Such voluntary initiatives are necessary in a democratic society, but they cannot be relied upon to replace government policy. Only governments can take the coercive actions that ensure structural justice to approximate fair equality of opportunity. Ad hoc volunteer efforts by civic institutions and private entities are important but insufficient.

STRUCTURAL JUSTICE BEYOND DIRECT POLICIES AND PRACTICES

Research

Fair equality of opportunity also requires research into areas where advancing knowledge will enhance the capabilities of persons and groups. The federal government, through agencies such as the NIH, FDA, and CDC, is needed to support advanced research that bolsters child development, therapy and treatment for various disabilities, public health needs, and changing circumstances to enable opportunities for persons with disabilities. States, for example, are unable to muster the research and political will informed by research to regulate guns that thwart security for some or to adequately comprehend environmental injustices in local communities. This continuing research is crucial to maintain fair equality of opportunity understood as fostering capability for opportunity, and it is a federal responsibility, which state and local governments and civic institutions are unable to fulfil other than on an ad hoc basis.

Even so, universities and nonprofits also have an important role in research that fosters capabilities for personal and group well-being. Consider child development studies and efforts to understand and treat health needs. These institutions are subject to civic pressures and free from some of the self-interested motives that limit research by for-profit entities, enabling them to promote research that expands capabilities. They still lack the wide perspective that can and sometimes does inform federal government research.

Basic research by pharmaceutical and medical device companies and other for-profit entities should not be ignored, but the profit motive, use of patents, and control of pricing mechanisms for "rent-seeking" on some products in poorly informed markets require regulation to maximize the benefits of these companies. Rent-seeking—a particularly destructive phenomenon according to Case and Deaton—occurs whenever private enterprises use their wealth to manipulate others to gain "profits" beyond the legitimate value of their initial entrepreneurial contributions. One vivid example occurs when pharmaceutical companies charge excessive fees for desperately needed drugs like insulin. Medicare, antitrust, and strict patent policies—along with regulation of advertising and lobbying—are needed to maximize the benefits of for-profit healthcare research.

Research that focuses on the effectiveness of therapies and practical remedies is also needed to extend the benefits of basic research. For example, what interventions in child development from beyond the family can best promote therapies and practices to enhance the capability of children with autism or Down's syndrome? What gun regulations are empirically demonstrated to effectively promote security and reduce deaths and injuries without restricting rights to self-defense and hunting? Here again, federally funded research is needed to promote public and private research to advance effective therapy and regulations. Federal agencies should review the effectiveness of their own programs.

Culture and Subcultures

Governments and civic and private institutions also have a role in changing cultural or subcultural influences that impede capability for opportunity. Consider how publicity about smoking cigarettes promoted public health or how public knowledge of women's contributions in the workplace freed women from confining subcultural norms. These changes can happen in two related ways.

First, new policies (e.g., paid parental leave for new mothers and fathers or laws permitting same-sex marriage) can change attitudes about common practices that limit or denigrate choices in a variety of arenas. These changes in culture also rely on research measuring the effectiveness of such policies, for example, the results for child development supported by stable same-sex parenting. Such changes in the culture can expand capabilities for different choices for well-being without detriment to opportunities for others.[2]

Second, government, as well as civic and private institutions, can offer public pronouncements that may change these cultural attitudes. We are accustomed to government and civic leaders praising values they believe expand and channel opportunities (e.g., praise for new opportunities for women or for LGBTQ persons). Governments and civic institutions need to be sensitive to the role culture has in forming values. Think of publicity as simple as lauding mothers' child-rearing work or vaccines that enhance our lives.

Culture sustains as well as thwarts the maternal role in the family and for different kinds of employment. Culture should preserve the freedom to form different kinds of families without impeding the role of the family in enhancing members' lives. Culture affects individual and family judgments about the kinds of employment that allow for parenting and even leisure time. Publicizing cultural values that make some women feel ill at ease in emphasizing their parental role or that denigrate female employees in some roles could limit the freedom of persons for family and employee roles. Diversity of cultural values should be protected in these arenas. We cannot say that this kind of publicity, whether promoted by governments or by civic and private institutions, can enable or thwart the capability for choices.

These observations contrast with the view that values are matters that can or should be left to individuals independently of the structures shaping culture. In fact, culture inevitably shapes individual decisions and behavior and is inevitably influenced by structural components emanating from institutions and governments. We need lively critical discussions about how laws and publicity shape our culture and what values governments and institutions promote, but we must recognize that structures, including those influenced by governments and their leaders, shape culture in ways that bear on our individual dispositions and actions. We should ask how governments and institutions shape the culture that necessarily expands or narrows individual, family, and small group opportunities for well-being. Laws and publicity shaped by institutions inevitably enable or restrict opportunity.

Conclusions Regarding Structural Justice and Opportunities

These areas, whether involving governments or civic and private institutions, forge structural changes that are in different ways and degrees coercive—and enabling—for individuals. They are necessary to foster choice and opportunities in various areas of our economic, civic, and family lives, thereby enhancing capabilities, freedom, and opportunity. Fair equality of opportunity requires structural justice that directs and demands individual responsibilities. Individuals and like-minded groups may comply with these structural demands with alacrity, but the structures remain necessary and, to some degree, coercive for those who do not consent. Some coercion is necessary. For example, taxes to provide paid paternity leave and universal daycare for young children should not be left to employers' discretion or volunteer donations. Individual choices about well-being and execution of our plans for well-being are insufficient.

INDIVIDUAL OBLIGATIONS

Individual compliance with structural requirements for fair equality of opportunity is needed but insufficient. Some responsibilities for fostering fair equality of opportunity require individual dispositions and behavior that go beyond compliance with structures. Compliance alone does not necessarily incorporate individual and associational dispositions that shape and extend mere obedience to laws. I have in mind responsibilities to foster the capability of family members, especially children but also seniors; responsibilities to encourage and even forgive friends and colleagues when they are broken by irresponsible behavior but ready to seek new opportunities; responsibilities to encourage persons broken by negative fate and lack of confidence; and obligations to initiate government and civic policies and practices that foster capability for others denied justice.

Parental responsibility for fostering the capability of children begins prenatally—regardless of one's views on the permissibility of abortion. Recent research shows that the brain development of fetuses depends on mothers avoiding alcohol and other drugs, their nutritional practices (especially avoiding iron deficiency), and their stress levels.[3] These practices to foster capability for prenatal children ultimately fall on parents, especially but not exclusively on mothers. That does not mean others are without responsibility or that structural justice has no role in child development. Partners, close family members, and friends have a role in encouraging and supporting mothers to refrain from alcohol and drug use and to practice good nutrition. Beyond individual responsibilities, structural justice is vital to these practices. Alcohol consumption is a good example. Research within the past fifty years was necessary to discover the effects of maternal alcohol consumption on the fetus. This research was backed by government and institutional funding. Moreover, these institutions have performed vital roles in publicizing these research findings and changing the culture regarding maternal care for the brain development of the fetus.

Parents also have responsibility for fostering capability for children, especially preschool children. Parents play a positive or negative role— and a vital one—in facilitating opportunities for their children. These responsibilities involve many dispositions and actions, ranging from nurturing cognitive and emotional development to avoiding transmitting stress to the child and, of course, any kind of child abuse. It may be appropriate to reiterate that these observations demonstrate that fair opportunity cannot be achieved by leaving children free to decide for themselves what goals to aspire to and pursue. Autonomy for children is not possible without parents as well as institutions fostering their capability for choice. These individual parental responsibilities must be supported by partners and friends and also by government policies such as paid maternity leave, a child tax credit, subsides and regulation of childcare, and even support for a stable, two-parent family structure.[4]

Structures to Support Parental Responsibility and Compensate When It Falters

We should keep two factors in mind regarding a two-parent family structure. First, evidence shows that the capability of children is not affected by the gender of the parents or in determinative ways by whether the parents are biological parents. Second, breakdowns in the stable two-parent family structure can be compensated for by government and individual practices, such as provision for payments for child support by an absent parent and for necessary support like childcare, healthcare, and education. Even though there is no fully adequate substitute for parental childcare, an institutional substitute can facilitate child capabilities.

Government has a clear role in supporting stable two-parent families and in providing vital compensatory help for parenting and children when the family structure breaks down. However, none of these qualifications on the benefits of a two-parent family structure contend that it is irrelevant to child development and opportunities for children. Nor do they specify which two-parent family structure is optimal for child development. Evidence suggests that same-sex parents are as effective as heterosexual parents.

Governments and civic institutions can also support parental health, especially mental health, in ways that nurture positive results for individual responsibility. Consider, for example, how parental anxiety can cause distress for the emotional development of children and how access to therapy can help parents reduce stress. Individual parent responsibility has an indispensable role for child development and mental health, but a structure that supports research, publicity, and therapy for the mental health of parents has a huge role in enabling parent-child relationships that expand opportunities for children.

Additional Obligations of Families, Colleagues, and Friends

Individual obligations for fair equality of opportunity of family members extend beyond children. It includes care, encouragement, and even forgiveness for siblings and aging members of the family whose capabilities have been diminished by changes in capacities and circumstances. These diminished capabilities include those from irresponsible behavior when the vestiges of that behavior render the person incapable of seizing new opportunities. Here again, structural justice has a role in fostering new capabilities, but in some cases only individuals with ongoing relationships can foster restored or modified capabilities. For example, senior living environments can provide a structure for nourishment, continuing friendships, and new learning, but these structures alone cannot foster capability that depends on interpersonal relations with siblings and children. As much as a government- or family-supported living environment can provide for the needs of an aging and declining person, the opportunity for that person to adjust to new realities and flourish as much as possible depends on communication and care from family members and friends. Individuals must initiate this fostering of capability for opportunities to choose and pursue the well-being for which seniors have a capacity.

These individual obligations for the justice of fair equality of opportunity are not limited to family members. They include colleagues in the workplace, civic organizations and religious groups, and friends. Once again, structural justice alone is not adequate to foster encouragement for a despondent colleague or friend, or to offer forgiveness for previous irresponsible action. Interpersonal forgiveness cannot be replaced by practices within incarceration or parole or post-incarceration that are also matters of justice for equal opportunity. Individual responsibility is insufficient yet indispensable in fostering these capabilities for opportunity.

More Individual Responsibilities

Individuals and small groups must also take responsibility for initiating efforts to bring about structural change when some persons and groups are vulnerable to opportunity deficits. These initiatives are often most effective if they enable vulnerable persons to speak and act for themselves. Inequalities of wealth and income can render some vulnerable groups nearly incapable of political action in a presumably democratic society. Individual citizens can and should take initiatives—often through civic or political organizations—to diminish inequalities that render vulnerable groups socially and politically powerless. Inequalities that follow from choices and by differences of merit in the workplace are not in and of themselves unjust in an equal opportunity society.

However, when they increase due to absence of fair inheritance taxes or regressive tax systems that place an unfair burden on those with grossly unequal income and wealth, these inequalities undermine the opportunity to participate effectively in the political process to achieve structural justice for equal opportunity. In these instances, all individual citizens have an obligation to initiate a movement for fairer tax policies.

Persons and groups deprived of fair equality of opportunity also have individual responsibility to advance justice for themselves. They may be vulnerable, but they are not without some capability for changing the structural order. Victims of injustice often understand their own circumstances better, if not perfectly, than others who act in their behalf or in coalition. In most cases, these persons, some types of disability or advanced age notwithstanding, are capable of contributing to initiatives to advance opportunity for themselves and others similarly situated. This optimism assumes that they have not been rendered powerless by gross inequalities of income, wealth, and political power. To the extent that they retain political capability, they have a special individual and group responsibility to act on their own behalf—and on behalf of the common good. The initiative of victims of unequal opportunity, when supported by others, is therapeutic and indispensable for effective change. Although eradicating unequal opportunity can never be left to the victims of injustice alone, collective effort by victims, supported by others, can effectively foster their capability for opportunity.

CONCLUSION

This book began with the goal of clarifying a generally accepted but poorly understood conception of equal opportunity. How does the conception of equality of opportunity proffered in this book differ from and correct common conceptions? How does it propose to advance justice in our society?

First, to reiterate: This conception of fair equality of opportunity to foster capability for persons and groups emphatically rejects equal opportunity reduced to selecting applicants based on the qualifications they bring to an application. Beyond qualifications, society must facilitate persons' capability to choose what outcomes they desire and become qualified for positions instrumental to those choices. That includes the capability to develop the requisite qualifications and, on occasion, to take affirmative action, adjusting criteria for qualification that we discover are themselves discriminatory—for example, SAT scores and GPA for higher education admission. An equal opportunity society must ensure every person the basic or minimal capability to choose what opportunities to seek and implement. Beyond minimal capability, it entails an equal capability to choose and seek positions and goals. Hence, when a racial, class, gender, or other distinct group is not represented in a particular status (e.g., educational achievement or income and wealth levels) in a relatively equal proportion with persons from other groups, we should seek to know the causes of the disproportion. They are often the capability deficits within that demographic group. Individual choices and irresponsible behavior explain why some persons from each group do not achieve outcomes as others do, but they do not adequately explain disproportional achievements in different groups. Capability deficits do; and to remedy these deficits, society must promote positive freedom (that is, the wherewithal) for all persons and groups to become qualified for the status they choose and seek. We must do what is necessary to enable all citizens to envision the possibilities for themselves and to become qualified to execute their choices.

Second, this conception of fair equality of opportunity differs from the view that responsible individuals and groups can ensure equal opportunity without structural changes wrought by government and other institutions. Behavior by individuals is insufficient to ensure fair equality of opportunity. We need changes in tax law, zoning regulations, provision for education, regulations for business and unions, the criminal justice system, and other institutional arrangements. In addition, structural reforms are needed to change cultural dispositions—for example, attitudes about the roles of women, about the likely success of gay and lesbian marriage, or about inherent lack of qualifications among some racial groups and classes. Structural changes are also needed to advance research required to enhance capability—for example, to overcome individual disabilities or child development deficits necessary for real opportunity. The latest development as I write is the use of electrodes in a forty-seven-year-old stroke victim's brain to enable her to communicate at eighty words per minute plus facial expressions via an avatar. It had been eighteen years since she had been able to communicate in language.[5]

Third, these structural reforms to satisfy justice do not enable complete equal opportunity, only its approximation consistent with maximizing opportunity for all. Persons with pervasive disabilities or other inveterate impediments to capability cannot always justly be raised to equal capability for choosing and executing opportunity. Sometimes this shortfall only means that persons cannot have identical capabilities; for example, I could not have become an All-Star baseball player like Ernie Banks. In other incidents, opportunities will be unequal for some, for example, a person ravaged by debilitating psychological or mental disabilities.

This conception of fair equality of opportunity does not claim injustice when outcomes are not identical or are in some circumstances unequal. Different and even unequal outcomes may be just. In fact, absolute equality of the value of outcomes may sometimes be *unjust* because it would rob some persons of opportunity by inordinate investments of time and money in others who are severely disabled or diminished by past behavior. This can happen when, for example, efforts are made to nurture fully equal opportunity for severely autistic persons that cause greater reductions in capability among others by depriving them of effective education or ordinary medical care. It can also occur when some are rescued from the throes of irresponsible behavior before they are ready to change. This caveat on the requirement for absolute equal capability never justifies neglecting prudent efforts to enhance the capability of every person, regardless of the seriousness of a person's dysfunctional condition or the reason for their condition.

Fourth, merit and qualifications count. While this book does not defend views of meritocracy based solely on individual responsibility, it does hold that the most qualified—or at least well-qualified—persons should be selected for positions and appointments and awarded according to their qualifications. Merit and qualifications count when justice ensures roughly equal capability for all, but honest assessment of qualifications remains inadequate independent of efforts to foster capability. This conception allows that irresponsible individual behavior leads to not only different but unequal results. Equal opportunity does not entail the view that all persons will achieve equal levels of well-being. However, we should be highly suspicious of disproportion outcomes by race, gender, disability, or other groups when these results are dubiously attributed to group irresponsibility or (except in some rare instances) to subcultural proclivities in preferences about what constitutes well-being. For example, it may be that women are more inclined to choose childcare or other forms of caring for family members that entails some sacrifice in some career achievements. It may be that some of them are maximizing well-being distinctive to them, but we should remain suspicious that structural arrangements in society—that is, the lack of paid maternity leave or the failure to provide a refundable child tax credit—heavily influences these supposedly preferred subcultural "choices."

Fifth, fair equality of opportunity is not a one-and-done achievement for a just starting line. Fair quality of opportunity should account for changes in choices and capabilities over a lifetime. It should also foster capabilities to overcome the vestiges of irresponsible behavior when persons indicate a readiness to take responsibility for new choices. These renewals of possibilities may be informed by religious views of grace and forgiveness incorporated into justice. That does not mean that they depend on sectarian justification. Grace and forgiveness as parts of justice are defensible from multiple religious and humanitarian perspectives. Indeed, a strong religious emphasis on retributive justice sometimes leaves less of a place for grace, forgiveness, and a hope for redemption than do humanitarian perspectives. It does mean that bringing persons to a starting line with equal capability is insufficient. Justice requires adjustments to changing circumstances in individuals' lives over time.

Sixth, the success or failure of fair equality of opportunity in society cannot be facilely measured by particular outcomes, for example, income levels, educational achievements, or a level of supposed career achievement. The conception of equal opportunity proposed here allows for—in fact requires—freedom of choice in what outcomes and conception of well-being persons pursue. While outcomes, astutely understood, can indicate a failure to achieve equal opportunity, efforts to associate equality of opportunity with specific preferred outcomes by an observer may deny people freedom (i.e., opportunity) to choose the outcomes they desire. For example, some will prefer a high school education and satisfying employment that does not demand a higher education degree. Some will be most content with leisure time and fishing that does not demand high-level employment with high income.

Seventh, the justice of equal opportunity requires individual responsibilities as well as structural change. This claim may involve parenting, forming families, instilling confidence in colleagues, and forgiving and encouraging friends and colleagues we deem to have been irresponsible. These individually responsible actions are not possible without structural supports, but structural justice alone is never fully adequate for fair equality of opportunity.

My hope is not that every reader will adopt this exact conception of equal opportunity but that these variations on some common conceptions will advance our discourse and sharpen our common thinking about what equal opportunity requires. I also hope this greater conceptional clarity will inform our policies, practices, and individual behavior to advance justice. The conception of equal opportunity advanced here certainly expands what is required by many current conceptions. It also falls short of those who contend for greater freedoms—for example, in family structure—or more equality of outcomes. We need to continue to refine our collective thinking on what is required by fair equality of opportunity, but my hope is that we can move beyond the "empty cliché" to which Steven Brill, whom I cite at the beginning of this book, refers. Perhaps it can also move us beyond the political and ideological polarization that currently paralyzes any hope for greater justice.

The question remains: To what extent does this conception of fair equality of opportunity entail the comprehensive demands of justice and of the moral life? I reserve that for a brief conclusion.

NOTES

1. See note 11 in chapter 3 and the James Heckman article cited there for one account of these well-researched preschool programs.

2. Laws and customs welcoming some practices—for example, driving without a seat belt, smoking in public, unrestricted availability of guns, or some unhealthy sexual behaviors—without chastising them, can expand some individual freedoms but reduce opportunities for many others. If we do not publicly denigrate forms of behavior that limit opportunities for many persons, cultural attitudes are likely to restrict opportunities. Once again, expanding opportunities does not follow from individual freedoms when they are detrimental to others. Social science research is key to understanding what cultural attitudes and dispositions promote or diminish the capability for opportunity.

3. My observations about these and other factors impacting on the development of children for which the children cannot be held responsible are informed by *Neurons to Neighborhoods*. (See chapter 3, note 1 for publication information.) It is more than incidentally relevant that the research on which this study was based was supported by grants from the US Congress and vetted by multiple private and public university researchers.

4. I have written about family structure and equal opportunity for children in another context. See "Fair Opportunity for Children and the Family," *International Encyclopedia of Ethics*, edited by Hugh LaFollette (Wiley-Blackwell, June 2017), DOI:10.1002/9781444367072.wbiee834, 1–12.

5. See S. L. Metzger et al. in *Nature* (2023), https://doi.org/10.1038/s41586-023-06443-4. A high-performance neuroprosthesis for speech decoding and avatar control.

Chapter 5

Alignment with a Comprehensive Conception of Justice and the Moral Life

Equality of opportunity, among those who affirm it as a part of justice, is normally understood as one part, often a small part, of a comprehensive view of justice. John Rawls, for example, proposes a separate first principle of liberty, and his "difference principle" seeks to secure greater equality of income and wealth than his fair equality of opportunity alone entails. The principle of liberty proposes to protect citizens and residents from coercive structures that limit the pursuit of ends they prefer. The difference principle prohibits inequalities that do not improve the absolute income or wealth position of the least well-off persons. The conception of fair equality of opportunity I propose here incorporates some of the concerns of Rawls's separate principles in modified ways but without directly engaging them. In short, the conception here is more comprehensive than Rawls—and more than many other conceptions of equal opportunity. It also resists the view of many who endorse much greater equality in outcomes than provided by this conception of equal opportunity. It allows for just inequalities of income, wealth, and other outcomes in circumstances where persons with equal capability choose contrasting outcomes. It also allows for at least short-term inequalities of outcomes when persons fail to execute due to irresponsible behavior. ("Short-term" because society is obligated to help persons recover from irresponsible behavior when they are ready to renew their lives.) In sum, fair equality of opportunity, as I present it, encapsulates many of the criteria normally incorporated in complete conceptions of justice as well as broader demands of some conceptions of the moral life, for example, an obligation to forgive.

INCORPORATES INDIVIDUAL LIBERTIES

A conception of fair equality of opportunity that approximates equal capability to choose and pursue any individual conception of well-being fully accounts for just liberties for persons and associated groups. It does, however, qualify individual liberties. It qualifies, of course, liberties to actively violate others but also liberties to ignore others' just claims for positive freedoms enabling fair opportunity. For example, it prohibits the liberty to reject or ignore adequate support for healthcare and public health or to ignore efforts—personal and structural—to foster citizens' and domestic residents' positive freedom to choose and execute their own choices about outcomes. It denies our freedom to ignore persons' struggles following incarceration or the need to help aging individuals cope with memory loss. It rejects freedom to ignore forgiving others when gracious forgiveness will enable their capability to function responsibly. It also rejects the freedom to pursue massive income and wealth while others are denied the equal capability to achieve the goals they desire. These individual claims to freedom are unjust. They violate fair equality of opportunity. Hence, fair equality of opportunity accounts for and guides the liberties that a full conception of justice demands.

Fair equality of opportunity protects the freedom of persons to pursue their own conception of well-being consistent with nurturing equal capability for all. It even affirms the freedom of persons who meet the demands of justice to reject generally preferred conceptions of well-being by other members of society. Citizens are free to choose their own preferred outcomes. There are no structural pressures to maximize education beyond high school and some training needed for modest employment. Persons are free to choose greater leisure or time devoted to child-rearing rather than working for higher-prestige jobs and higher wages for their well-being. Achieving outcomes is not measured by income, wealth, or job status, which some wrongly equate with greater opportunities. Fair equality of opportunity even leaves persons free not to advance a vision of the common good insofar as this common good is not necessary to promote equal capability for others' opportunity.

On the other hand, failures to comply with and even to support a healthy environment and long-term climate necessary for opportunities for all are unjust according to this conception of fair equality of opportunity. So are freedoms to adopt unhealthy practices, such as resisting scientifically proven vaccines for contagious diseases. These latter freedoms jeopardize the liberty and equal opportunity of others, as well as risk the health of those who adopt them. These situations can become complex when adult family members choose not to wear seat belts or consume excessive calories when other family members are dependent on their good health. Beneficiaries of equal opportunity are normally free to choose less than maximum health for themselves but not free to jeopardize others' capability for health. In sum, just freedoms to choose and pursue a conception of well-being are incorporated in this conception of fair equality of opportunity, but these freedoms should not detract from the capability of others to pursue their well-being.

EQUALITY OF OUTCOMES

Fair equality, as conceived above, also covers the concerns of Rawls's difference principle for greater equality of income and wealth than his principle of fair equality of opportunity provides. What's more, it accounts for equalities of other outcomes that some proponents of justice incorporate within their conceptions of justice. Recall that inequalities of income and wealth are not the only group or individual outcomes that fair equality of opportunity addresses. It also addresses unequal education, housing, security, meaningful work experiences, criminal justice, and even participation in political and civic affairs when the capability for opportunity is not assured some demographic groups.

It examines injustices that lead to disproportional outcomes among groups. Even though different individual outcomes are easily and justly explained by individuals' freedom to choose different outcomes or by individual irresponsible behavior (often temporary), disproportionate unequal outcomes among groups are inconsistent with fair equality of opportunity. Only in the rarest instances can disproportionate group outcomes in higher education or high-status and high-paying jobs be consistent with individual freedom. Although some African Americans, other minorities, and some immigrants no doubt choose less education or lower-status employment or act irresponsibly in pursuing their ends, there is no reason—except past and continuing inequalities of capability—that disproportionate numbers of these groups experience these results. This conception of fair equality of opportunity calls for remedies to these unjust inequalities. I have observed that in extreme cases, some of these disproportionate inequalities may occur for disabled persons or, in rare cases, for women, but we should be suspicious. These inequalities frequently result from unjustly diminished capabilities, sometimes even attributable to unjustly shaped sub-cultures. At the time of this writing, many mothers are remaining outside of the workforce, not by their choice but because the cost of childcare prohibits employment that would force them to leave children without adequate care.

In sum, concern for just equality of outcomes as proposed by the conception of fair equality of opportunity in this book is much more comprehensive than a conception of equal opportunity that focuses principally on income and wealth. It includes factors pertaining to equal capability for all outcomes and for all groups that disproportionately fall short of outcomes commonly chosen by other groups. Education levels and health and longevity in life among Blacks and working-class persons of all races offer good examples.

JUST INEQUALITIES OF OUTCOMES

Fair equality of opportunity allows for some unequal outcomes. It also assumes that these outcomes can be acceptable—even affirmed—within the most comprehensive standards of justice. If persons are assured equal capability for pursuing opportunities and either choose outcomes that lead to inequalities in one sphere or another or fail to responsibly pursue the outcomes they choose, the inequalities of outcomes are just. They may also include inequalities—not always limited to income—that incentivize some to undertake onerous work that benefits many. This is a modified version of Rawls's difference principle.

These inequalities may sometimes be further reduced by acts of charity and kindness, but justice can be consistent with some inequalities. These inequalities should never exceed different outcomes that might be chosen by capable persons or that might be explained by irresponsible behavior. Inequalities should have adequate explanations consistent with fair equality of opportunity. For example, when Blacks or women are disproportionally unemployed or in unequal positions in the workplace, we need explanations for how these inequalities are justified or caused by specific injustices that we can then remedy.

RENEWAL AND REGENERATION

There is another area in which this conception of fair equality of opportunity varies from more typical conceptions. It insists that, both structurally and interpersonally, equal opportunity provide for renewal or forgiveness for those who need capabilities to make changes in their lives. For example, a person who decides she wants to study to be a lawyer or a tree pruner later in life should have the capability to make that change. Similarly, a person struggling to overcome the consequences of even a just incarceration should be granted the resources and forgiveness to renew his life with new choices and behavior. This view of justice and equal opportunity accounts for grace and forgiveness that are sometimes considered matters of religious faith, not of universal justice. But I have argued that grace and forgiveness can be justified within many religious traditions as well as by humanistic moral thought. I hope I have shown that judgment, grace, and forgiveness leading to redemption from irresponsible conduct are dispositions that many religious and humanistic persons find convincing.

We might expand these obligations to persons who have conducted their lives irresponsibly a step further. First, there is an implied obligation in the conception of fair equality of opportunity to express an effective and judicious negative judgment toward the irresponsible person. The judgment toward an irresponsible person may help protect the victims of his behavior and be an act of grace if it helps the irresponsible person redeem himself. This obligation is both to the person acting irresponsibly and to those who can be negatively affected by his irresponsible behavior. Consider the children, spouses, and close friends of persons whose relationships have been disrupted by just incarceration.

The negatively affected can and should also be encouraged to offer, when the timing is appropriate, forgiveness that heals. This exercise of forgiveness can be especially effective when it originates with groups harmed by the irresponsible behavior. Such forgiveness can foster capability for restored opportunities as well as for improved relationships that others need.

Both the obligations to judge others effectively and to forgive demonstrate that the demands of fair equality of opportunity should not be narrowly conceived in terms of isolated individual practices alone. These obligations can be collective actions. Consider the forgiveness and call to justice enacted by Mother Emmanuel AME Church in Charleston, South Carolina. In that case, the then-US president and the congregation acted collectively, offering both judgment and forgiveness that bolstered the capability of many.

PERSONAL MORAL DEMANDS
INCORPORATED INTO JUSTICE

Justice as understood in this conception of fair equality of opportunity is comprehensive in respect to demands on individual behavior as well as structural policy. Family members, especially parents, and colleagues and friends have an indispensable role to play in achieving equal opportunity and justice. We are also required as individual citizens to work for structural changes that expand fair equality for all. On this view, many demands on the individual moral life are incorporated into justice so that much of what is required of us morally is also required for us to act justly. The demands on individuals to achieve fair equality of opportunity go well beyond the singularly structural approach by Rawls and many other philosophical conceptions of equal opportunity.

MORE TO THE MORALITY, SOME
OF WHICH BEARS ON JUSTICE

This robust conception of fair equality of equal opportunity covers most of what justice demands of us in our society. It does not incorporate the entirety of the moral life or what justice demands in different spheres, for example, criminal justice for the sake of bringing violators to account or justice beyond our border. Nor does it consider moral judgments about practices—for example, involvement in civic affairs, the type of education we pursue, and even the decision whether to abort a fetus—that rightly extend beyond the law or coercive intuitions. There are also complicated decisions about when and how to judge and when and how to forgive (others and ourselves). These decisions should not be coerced by law, but they are subject to moral judgments.

Fair equality of opportunity as I have conceived it applies only to domestic affairs in the United States, although it considers what we owe to immigrants, refugees, and asylees the same thing we owe to citizens. Equality of opportunity also entails obligations beyond our borders, although not the same that we owe, either structurally or personally, to those within our borders. We—and our government and institutions—have obligations to global citizens (e.g., among the Ukrainians in Central Asia; the Uyghurs in China; Palestinians and Jewish citizens of Israel, the West Bank, and Gaza; and the Rohingyas in Myanmar), but those obligations should be adjusted to the realities of different possibilities when we are less in control. They also must also be adjusted to the realities of prudent practices and policies accounting for the lack of authority and proximity relative to global citizens. I do not deny, nor do I consider, the justice of these demands on us and our institutions. We should attend to these matters of justice, but I do not think that alters the equal opportunity we owe to our fellow citizens and residents and those seeking immigrant status in our nation.

We also have moral obligations to others and to the common good that are not entailed by justice. This book does not consider the demands of the moral life beyond justice: obligations to the common good only indirectly related to equal opportunity, obligations to care for family and neighbors that exceed what equal opportunity requires. Here again, these moral judgments should not be legally binding. Some laudably sense a moral obligation to be the best possible at their work or in other endeavors—significant moral obligations that we would not codify or incorporate into a conception of fair equality of opportunity.

Despite the comprehensiveness of this conception of fair equality of opportunity, some aspects of justice and of the moral life remain beyond its reach.

CONCLUSION

My hope is that this book proffers a conception and defense of equality of opportunity that pushes us beyond both a facile cliché and a narrow conception that omits fostering capability that sometimes plagues our thinking about justice. I do not expect universal concurrence but hope this conception of fair equality of opportunity moves us toward a more reasoned examination of what equal opportunity requires of our societal structures and of us as individuals and associated communities. It also advocates for a disposition toward others and seeks to account for their circumstances. It demonstrates the need for social scientific considerations without engaging fine points of social scientific disputes; it is not limited to principles or explicit guidelines for moral judgments. Even general agreement about this broad conception would not of course assure us a just society, but in our polarized world, it would help us focus on principles and issues that could move us toward that end.

Bibliography for Further Reading

Abramitzky, Ran, and Leah Boustan. *Streets of Gold: America's Untold Story of Immigrant Success.* New York: Hachette Book Group, 2022.

Beckley, Harlan. "Capability as Opportunity: How Amartya Sen Revises Equality of Opportunity." In *Journal of Religious Ethics* 30/1 (Spring 2002): 107–35.

———. "Ethics and Advocacy in Pedagogy: An Example in Poverty Studies." In *Ethics and Advocacy: Bridges and Boundaries*, ed. by Harlan Beckley et al. Eugene, OR: Cascade Books, 2022.

———. "Fair Opportunity for Children and the Family." In *International Encyclopedia of Ethics*, ed. by Hugh LaFollette. Hoboken, NJ: Wiley-Blackwell, June 2017.

Blank, Rebecca M. *It Takes a Nation: A New Agenda for Fighting Poverty.* Princeton, NJ: Princeton University Press, 1997.

Case, Anne, and Angus Deaton. *Deaths of Despair and the Future of Capitalism.* Princeton, NJ: Princeton University Press, 2020.

Chetty, Raj. "Opportunity Insights." Available at https://opportunityinsights .org.

Daniels, Norman. *Just Health: Meeting Health Needs Fairly.* New York: Cambridge University Press, 2008

Desmond, Matthew. *Evicted: Poverty and Profit in the American City.* New York: Broadway Books, 2016.

———. *Poverty, By America.* New York: Crown, 2023.

Duncan, Greg, and Suzanne Le Menestrel. *Consensus Study Report of the National Academy of Sciences, A Roadmap to Reducing Poverty.* Washington, DC: The National Academy Press, 2019.

Duncan, Greg J., and Richard Murnane. *Restoring Opportunity: The Crisis of Inequality and the Challenge for American Education.* Cambridge, MA: Harvard University Press, 2014.

————, eds. *Whither Opportunity? Rising Inequality, Schools, and Children's Life Chances*. New York: Russell Sage Foundation, 2011.

Dworkin, Ronald. "What Is Equality? Part 2: Equality of Resources." In *Philosophy & Public Affairs* 10/4 (1981): 283–345.

DeParle, Jason. *American Dream: Three Women, Ten Kids, and a Nation's Drive to End Welfare*. New York: Viking, 2004.

Faden, Ruth, and Madison Powers. *Structural Injustice: Power, Advantage, and Human Rights.* New York: Oxford University Press, 2019.

Haggerty, Rosanne. "Community Solutions." Available at https://www.youtube .com/watch?v=ca_N4vWnVnM&list=PLXEYyGucbAbqsBuS2otsVLgnsk C3yhOc7&index=1&t=21s.

Heckman, James, et al. "Early Childhood Education." Available at https:// heckmanequation.org/www/assets/2017/01/FINALMoffitt-ECE-Paper2015 .pdf.

Hicks, Douglas A. "Gender, Discrimination, and Capability: Insights from Amartya Sen." In *Journal of Religious Ethics* 30/1 (Spring 2002): 137–54.

National Research Council Institute of Medicine. *From Neurons to Neighborhoods: The Science of Early Childhood Development.* Washington, DC: National Academy Press, 2000.

Nussbaum, Martha C., and Jonathan Glover, eds. *Women, Culture and Development*. New York: Oxford University Press, 1995.

Nussbaum, Martha C., and Amartya Sen, eds. *The Quality of Life*. Oxford, UK: Clarendon Press, 1993.

Pew Charitable Trust and Russell Sage Foundation. "Economic Mobility in the United States." Available at https://www.pewtrusts.org/~/media/assets/2015 /07/fsm-irs-report_artfinal.pdf.

Rawls, John. *A Theory of Justice*. Revised edition. Cambridge, MA: Belknap Press of Harvard University Press, 1999.

————. *Political Liberalism*. Expanded edition. New York: Columbia University Press, 2005.

Roemer, John E. *Equality of Opportunity*. Cambridge, MA: Harvard University Press, 1998.

Rothstein, Richard. *The Color of Law: A Forgotten History of How Our Government Segregated America.* New York: W. W. Norton & Company, 2017

Sandel, Michael J. *The Tyranny of Merit: What's Become of the Common Good*. New York: Farrar, Straus, and Giroux, 2020.

Sen, Amartya. *Development as Freedom*. New York: Alfred A. Knopf, 1999.

————. *Inequality Reexamined.* Cambridge, MA: Harvard University Press, 1992

————. "Justice: Means versus Freedoms." In *Philosophy and Public Affairs* 19/2 (Spring 1990): 111–21.

Shipler, David K. *The Working Poor: Invisible in America.* New York: Alfred A. Knopf, 2004.

Sypnowich, Christine. *Equality Renewed: Justice, Flourishing and the Egalitarian Ideal.* New York and London: Routledge, 2017.

———. "Is Equal Opportunity Enough?" Published in a "Forum" essay of the *Boston Review,* a reader-funded website at letters@bostonreview.net.

Western, Bruce. *Punishment and Inequality in America.* New York: Russell Sage, 2006.

———. *Homeward: Life in the Year After Prison.* New York: Russell Sage, 2018.

Wooldridge, Adrian. *The Aristocracy of Talent: How Meritocracy Made the Modern World.* New York: Skyhorse Publishing, 2021.

Index

161

About the Author

Harlan Beckley grew up on a farm in central Illinois before attending the University of Illinois to study economics. He holds a master of divinity degree and a PhD in theological ethics at Vanderbilt University. He came to Washington and Lee University in 1974 and served as a teacher and administrator until his retirement in 2014. He founded the Thomas and Nancy Shepherd Program for the study of poverty and human capability in 1997 and the Shepherd Higher Education Consortium on Poverty in 2012.

Harlan served in multiple appointments and received recognitions from Washington and Lee and at the state and national levels, including an honorary doctorate in 2018.

Harlan and his spouse, Debby, parented three children (Ben, Jon, and Rachel), to whom this book is dedicated. They continue to reside in Lexington, Virginia.

Printed in the USA
CPSIA information can be obtained
at www.ICGtesting.com
LVHW091738080524
779614LV00002B/320